THE SOUTHERN WA

CW00481207

CONTENTS

© Kevin Robertson (Noodle Books) and the various contributors 2008

ISBN 978-1-906419-05-9

First published in 2008 by Kevin Robertson
under the **NOODLE BOOKS** imprint
PO Box 279
Corhampton
SOUTHAMPTON
SO32 3ZX
www.kevinrobertsonbooks.co.uk

Printed in England by
Ian Allan Printing Ltd
Hersham, Surrey

Editorial Introduction

January 1858 witnessed the opening of the first section of main line of the erstwhile LCDR, between Canterbury and Faversham. Subsequent openings, together with the numerous branch lines, followed, with the main line completed throughout by 1861.

To commemorate this anniversary we are delighted to present a photographic tribute of the last days of steam working, which occurred half a century ago, as seen through the camera of Alan Postlethwaite,

Going back further in time further it is with a little bit of tongue in cheek that I have included the piece on the legacy of Mr Price. Here are some wonderful photographs taken as a result of a tragic accident. The dilemma may be thus, does the fact that we wish to view the material from a railway and historic perspective in any way compromise the incident itself? I sincerely hope no one will see it that way.

As most of you will be aware, from 2009 we shall be going to what I hope will be a regular four issues a year. I say hope, as there is an amount of work to undertake for each issue, whilst we have also given a considerable amount of thought to the scheduling involved. The first ideas was to try to condense the issues with two in the spring and two in the autumn and thus coincide with the various shows. By doing so, however, I am conscious both of people's pockets and also the result of four issues appearing in quick succession between autumn 2009 and the spring of the next year.

The result is that we shall be conventional, January, April, July and October in 2009. Obviously we will also monitor the results carefully and any change, if deemed necessary, will be given as much notice as possible.

Again, though, I ask for your feedback. Please let me know your opinion as regarding these timescales.

What I can say is that *Southern Way* will never ascribe to more than four issues a year. How some do a monthly magazine manage on their own, I cannot imagine!

What I must also apologise for is not being able to commit to producing a particular article at the intended time. I promise you the intentions are genuine, but the practicalities are not always so and, in consequence, we have several major pieces that would have been ideal in 2008 but which will now appear in 2009.

Occasionally too, someone will come up with an idea on which, not only do I have no knowledge but I cannot think of anyone else who might either. So, if you know of anyone with a special knowledge of Crystal Palace, or the proposed transfer of steam engines to the IOW to replace the O2s, and I don't mean the 84xxx class either, please let me know!

As I have mentioned previously, the 'Preview' Issue of 'SW' sold out in the autumn of last year. Issue 1 almost followed, whilst No 2 was similarly down to just double figures. Heartened that I am, of course, it left me with a dilemma. Do we allow all three to disappear from the shelves and try to run a series with just No 3 and subsequent issues, or do we reprint all three titles? The latter was the eventual decision, so if anyone is missing the earlier issues they should be available again for a little while.

Finally, as this is the last issue of 2008, may I be the first to wish you the compliments of the season. I can almost hear you groaning as a result, but, just remember, by the time your read this in September, the decorations will also be on sale in the supermarkets. At that I am groaning as well.

Kevin Robertson

Left - A scene it would be almost possible to replicate today. Swanage 1965, by Rod Hoyle, of course.

Preceding page - Bournemouth Central, 2.15 pm, on an unknown day in July 1951. Platform 1, that for down trains and arrivals from Waterloo is deserted, but certainly not so Platform 3. Here the throng could well be waiting for a Waterloo service, possibly the 2.25 FO working or 2.35 daily working - if we knew the date. Amongst the fixtures and fitting the style of loudspeaker and lampshade were common throughout the system. Originally known as Bournemouth East, this was part of the route from Ringwood - see page 33 in this issue. Nowadays trains no longer arrive from Ringwood, whilst this is also the only station carrying the name Bournemouth. It is also minus the centre two sets of rails.

Front cover - Urie 'H16' No 30519 at of course Clapham Junction. This engine, together with others of the class were employed on ECS workings between Clapham and Waterloo from about 1951 onwards, although Bradley refers to the type soon being prohibited from running bunker first into the Terminus - any ideas why? It survived until November 1962. Paul Hersey collection
Rear cover - Wokingham. Jeffrey Grayer

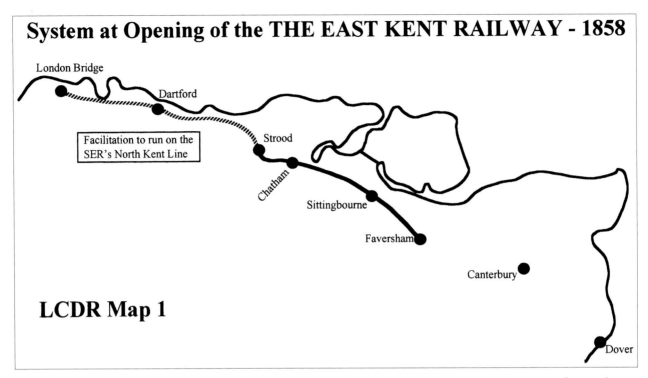

System at Opening of the THE EAST KENT RAILWAY - 1858

London Bridge
Dartford
Facilitation to run on the SER's North Kent Line
Strood
Chatham
Sittingbourne
Faversham
Canterbury
Dover

LCDR Map 1

Map 1. The original name of the London, Chatham and Dover Railway was the East Kent Railway. The first section opened in 1858 between Faversham and Strood, feeding into the South Eastern Railway's North Kent line, which had opened nine years earlier. The SER could have absorbed the EKR, but it chose not to and gave priority to its own trains on the overcrowded line to London Bridge. So the EKR remained independent and went ahead with its Western Extension to London, which was authorised in 1858. (This EKR should not be confused with the later EKR, a light railway that served the Kent coalfield.)

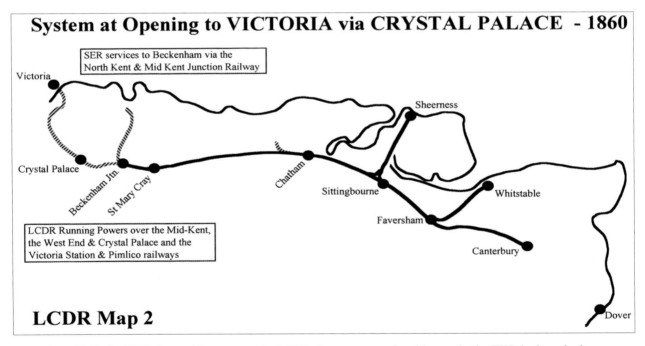

System at Opening to VICTORIA via CRYSTAL PALACE - 1860

SER services to Beckenham via the North Kent & Mid Kent Junction Railway
Victoria
Sheerness
Crystal Palace
Beckenham Jtn.
St Mary Cray
Chatham
Sittingbourne
Whitstable
LCDR Running Powers over the Mid-Kent, the West End & Crystal Palace and the Victoria Station & Pimlico railways
Faversham
Canterbury
Dover

LCDR Map 2

Map 2. In 1860, the EKR changed its name to the LCDR. In two years of rapid growth, the EKR had reached Canterbury, Whitstable and Sheerness and had finished its Western Extension over the North Downs to St Mary Cray. To reach Victoria, the 'Chatham' had running powers and paid tolls to: the Mid-Kent (Bromley & St Mary Cray) Railway, the West End & Crystal Palace Railway, and the Victoria & Pimlico Railway. (This Mid-Kent line should not be confused with the other one through Catford Bridge which was worked by the SER and whose name endured into the BR era.)

THE 150ᵗʰ ANNIVERSARY OF THE LONDON, CHATHAM & DOVER RAILWAY

The Development of the LCDR System - a photographic tribute

Alan Postlethwaite

To the 'Chatham' - 150 years old and still admired - Invicta!

The SR rationalised the two Victorias in 1923. The 'Brighton' station is seen here on the left with its grand overall roof. On the more mundane 'Chatham' side, 'Battle of Britain' class Pacific No. 34087 *145 Squadron* is standing in Continental platform 8, known as the 'Gateway to the Continent'. A fireman fits headcode discs while the driver chats to station staff.

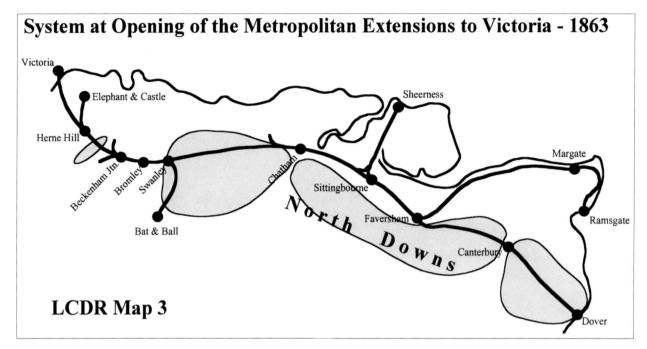

System at Opening of the Metropolitan Extensions to Victoria - 1863

LCDR Map 3

Map 3. In 1863, the LCDR took over the Mid-Kent and opened its Metropolitan Extensions from Penge junction to London. Trains divided at Herne Hill for Victoria and the City, the latter opening in 1863 as far as Elephant & Castle. The LCDR had also reached Dover, Ramsgate and Sevenoaks. The main line was a switchback, passing over or through the North Downs three times and through the difficult clay of Penge tunnel. During the international financial crisis of the late 1860s, there was an attempted redemption of debenture stock which the LDCR was unable to pay, causing bankruptcy of the Chatham's main contractor who was a principal stockholder. Intense competition with the SER impoverished both companies further and led to their eventual merger.

Opposite upper - Island platform 1 & 2 at Victoria becomes narrow at the end. Platform 1 (right) was originally dual-gauge for the use of Great Western trains working via the West London line. Class N Mogul, No. 31413 prepares to take empty stock to Eardley sidings via Herne Hill, Tulse Hill and Streatham. The SR barrow is for taking tail-lamps to the buffer stop end.

Opposite lower - Platform 1 at Victoria has a tall scenic backdrop of terraced residences. Champing at the bit, 'King Arthur' class 4-6-0 No. 30777 *Sir Lamiel* awaits the right of way. The signal box is SECR, extended by the SR for power signalling.

Right - The Metropolitan Extensions run mostly on viaducts. The line from Victoria splits at Brixton into the Catford Loop (right) and the Herne Hill line (left). Class W 2-6-4 tank, No. 31912, is en route to Hither Green marshalling yard with a heavy freight. The tall, baroque LCDR signal box had recently closed, superseded by power signalling.

Left - The Herne Hill line through Brixton passes under the South London line of the LBSCR. The skew bridge is of LCDR design and construction. 'Battle of Britain' class Pacific No. 34088 *213 Squadron* heads a train to the Channel ports via Tonbridge. The Camp coffee is optional.

Centre - In a display of smoke, steam and power, a heavy freight train approaches Herne Hill station from the Down sorting sidings. It is headed by class N Mogul No. 31410 and an illegible 0-6-0 class Q1.

Lower - Penge tunnel took over 3 years to build. It is a mile and a quarter long, bored through London clay and lined with bricks baked from its own spoil. Because of smoke obscuration within, repeater distant signals were provided at either end. At Sydenham Hill, class D1 4-4-0 No. 31749 runs light into the sunshine.

Opposite top - At Sydenham Hill, 'Schools' class 4-4-0 No. 30938, *St Olaves,* heads a train of train of BR Mark 1 stock in crimson and cream, en route to Ramsgate. The signal box is by Saxby & Farmer.

Looking north from the old island platform at Ludgate Hill, the triple roof of Holborn Viaduct terminus is far right. The lines under the LCDR signal box descend steeply through Snow Hill station to the Widened Lines of the Metropolitan. On the right, the lattice post and finial are LCDR, fitted with an SR yard lamp.

Left - Blackfriars Bridge station opened in 1864, south of the Thames. When the second Alexandra Bridge opened in 1885, this fine station became goods-only. Class E1 4-4-0 No. 31507 stands outside one of the old sheds. It is about to take over duty on an RCTS special train from Liverpool Street to Gravesend West - out via East Finchley, return via the East London line.

Centre - The 'Chatham' side of Peckham Rye was in the baroque style of the LBSCR. The LBSCR built both lines between Peckham and Loughborough and the LCDR built both lines between Loughborough and Battersea. Heading a freight train from Hither Green is Wainwright class C 0-6-0 No. 31317.

Lower - To serve the relocated Great Exhibition, no expense was spared for the LCDR terminus at Crystal Palace. The brickwork was ornate and massive for the tunnel portal and the cutting abutment. Opened in 1865, the line was electrified in 1925. The Palace burnt down in 1936 and the branch closed in 1954.

Opposite top - Lattice posts and arrowhead finials were characteristic of SECR signal assemblies. These brackets, with co-acting arms, are guarding Bickley junction. Work was ongoing in 1959 to quadruple the line to Swanley and to ease the curves on the spurs to the SER. Having bowed ends in the style of the LSWR, 4-SUB Unit No. 4303 (originally 3-SUB) was an early EMU built by the Southern.

Right - An unidentified 'Schools' class 4-4-0 approaches Swanley with a train from Chatham. Civil engineering work is in hand for impending colour-light signalling and to change the track designations through Swanley from Up-Up-Down-Down to Up-Down-Up-Down. The original LCDR station was sited at the junction itself (just to the right here) before relocation by the SR.

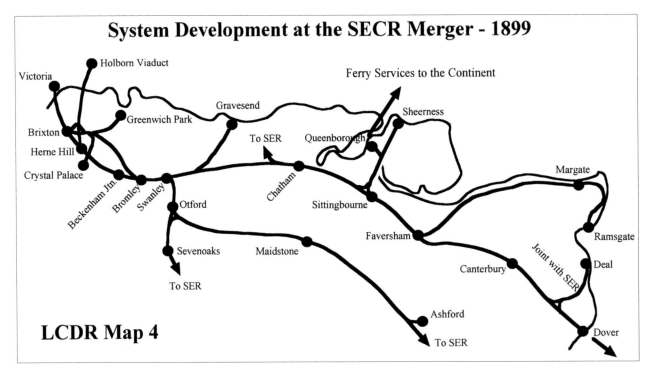

System Development at the SECR Merger - 1899

LCDR Map 4

Map 4. In 1899. The LCDR and SER merged operationally to become the South Eastern & Chatham Railway. By that time, the LCDR had reached Maidstone, Ashford, Gravesend and Deal and operated Continental ferry services out of Dover and (with breaks) from Queenborough (originally Sheerness). The SECR rationalised lines and services and became part of the Southern Railway at the grouping in 1923.

Above - The LCDR line to Ashford opened in 1884. It connected with the SER and had its own terminus, known latterly as Ashford West. Upon the SECR merger in 1899, the terminus became goods-only. The old carriage shed is seen here on the left. The grassy platforms once had canopies.

Right - The eastern end of Chatham is murky and congested with canopies, a road bridge, a tunnel portal, iron brackets, old gas lamps, new colour-lights, EMU stop signs and small piles of debris. With its tall Riddles tender, standard class 4MT 4-6-0 No. 75066 awaits the green light.

Left - LCDR lines were electrified to Gillingham, Maidstone and Sevenoaks by 1939. Electrification was extended to the coast in 1959, followed by Maidstone to Ashford in 1960, making Maidstone East one of the last outposts of LCDR steam. This crew is watering and bunker-trimming BR standard class 4MT 2-6-4 tank No. 80087 on an Up train, prior to crossing the Medway bridge.

Left - At Sittingbourne, a fireman fills the tank of class C 0-6-0 No. 31495. It will then run round Set No. 953 of BR Mark 1 stock before another trip to Sheerness. It seems not to matter that this was a goods engine, for this was the last day of steam hereabouts.

Centre - Near Faversham, class N Mogul No. 31824 cuts through grasses and wild flowers with a Continental mixed bag of vans from Bricklayers Arms, running via Chislehurst and Chatham to Dover. This was the very first section of the East Kent Railway to be opened in 1858, Faversham to Chatham on 25 January followed by Chatham to Strood on 13 March.

Bottom - Still wearing its air-smoothed casing, 'West Country' class Pacific No. 34101 *Hartland* drifts through a wooded cutting with a boat train to Victoria.

Opposite lower - A footbridge over the Thanet line gives a splendid view of Faversham junction. A train of pure Maunsell composition is headed by class N Mogul No. 31861, a 'Woolworths' engine made at Woolwich Arsenal. The marshalling yard (right) served the Faversham Creek branch and the Shepherd Neame brewery. The MPD (left) holds several Ivatt tanks, while new EMUs wait ominously beyond.

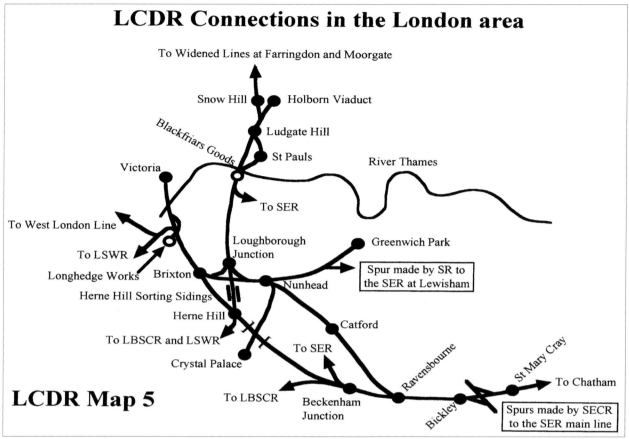

Map 5. In the London area, the LCDR opened the Crystal Palace branch in 1865, the Greenwich branch in 1871 - 1888 and the Catford Loop in 1892, the latter creating a second route between Bromley and London. In 1914, the SECR built spurs to the SER main line at Bickley and St Mary Cray. The SR rationalised the Thanet lines in 1926 and built the Lewisham spur in 1929, facilitating cross-London freight between West London and Hither Green yard. The LCDR's works and a goods station were at Longhedge. There were junctions with the LSWR and the West London line at Longhedge and with the LBSCR at Herne Hill, (facilitating LSWR services from Wimbledon). Sorting sidings at Herne Hill served the LCDR's city goods station at Blackfriars Bridge, (south of the Thames). This was also a passenger terminus until superseded by Ludgate Hill and Holborn Viaduct. There was a spur to the SER at Blackfriars and a subterranean connection to the Widened Lines at Farringdon and Moorgate to the Metropolitan, Midland and Great Northern railways. This north-south link survives today as Thameslink.

This page top - Ramgate Harbour terminus opened in 1863 and closed in 1926 as part of the rationalisation of Thanet. In 1959, a fairground occupied the site. There was once a turntable at Merrie England and a small loco yard by the helter skelter. The tunnel approach was on the right. Anyone for whelks?

This page centre - At Canterbury East, King Arthur's plume stands out against a stormy sky. Class N15 4-6-0 No. 30769 *Sir Balan* awaits the green flag with a Up train. The signal post is SR - rail-built with a flat cap.

This page bottom - Pride of the Bulleid fleet and first of its breed, 'Merchant Navy' class Pacific No. 35001 *Channel Packet* bursts through Dover Priory with a boat train to Victoria. Alongside, Fairburn 2-6-4 tank No. 42076 stands with a local train.

Opposite top - The LCDR's Dover Harbour station opened in 1861 and closed in 1927. Passing through in 1959 is 'The Man of Kent', an evocative name for a tortuous service between Margate and Charing Cross via Ramsgate, Deal, Folkestone and Tonbridge. It is headed here by 'West Country' class Pacific No. 34014 *Budleigh Salterton*, signalled to take the Hawkesbury curve onto the SER. Dover's Western Docks are to the right.

Opposite lower left - SS *Shepperton Ferry* was one of the Southern's coal-fired train ferries which was commissioned in 1936 for the Dover-Dunkirk service. It could accommodate 12 sleeping cars and some 40 goods wagons or up to 100 motor cars. It is moored at Admiralty Pier which opened in 1860 and closed to passengers in 1919 when Dover Marine opened. This was the terminus for LCDR tidal boat trains.

Opposite lower right - On a quite different scale, the wharf at Blackfriars Bridge had a wagon turntable and a small jib crane. A painted 'Southern Railway' sign was semi-legible in 1960 but the LCDR insignia and crest had been cast in iron to be read until eternity. So let us toast this impudent upstart of a railway that gave the SER a run for its money but never paid a penny of dividend to its ordinary shareholders: 'Invicta'.

The 1932
BRIGHTON LINE RESIGNALLING
PART 2
(Continued from Issue 3, Spring 2008)

Shunt signals, in the form of small units attached to the appropriate signal or mounted at ground level and displaying only red or green, allowed movement either as far as the next signal or as far as the line was clear. Two examples of this would be No 16 or No 17 at Preston Park, where the green aspect permitted movement to either two or three separate destinations, although only a single indication of green was given. This was typical of Southern practice for many years. This varies from current practice, where a visual display, advising the driver which route he was to take, would normally now be provided in addition to the indication to proceed. 'Limit of Shunt' boards, represented by the letter 'K' within a square, were also provided where necessary.

At the same location the down branch advanced starting signal, Preston Park No 22, would clear to a yellow aspect when only Preston Park No 22 was reversed. The green aspect was displayed when both the levers for Preston Park No 22 and Hove East's semaphore home signal had been reversed. The semaphore arm also had to be proved to be 'off' in the electrical circuit.

Some renaming of lines also took place in the Brighton area at this time. The previous terms 'down main' and 'up main' were now referred to as 'down through' and 'up through', whilst the former spur lines on the Cliftonville Curve were re-designated the 'up' and 'down' branch. From Brighton, the route west towards Hove was now referred to as the 'down west branch' and the Lewes route the 'down east branch'. The up lines from these respective points were similarly renamed.

Coming from Hove, the bracket signal containing the four semaphore arms was fitted with approach lights similar to those at Keymer Junction referred to previously. Additionally, the two arms permitting trains to take the Holland Road line were provided with the facility to display double yellow as well as the single yellow or green aspects. This was necessary due to the restricted braking distances between this point and the following two signals, Nos 167 and 173.

An exception to the earlier comment about the use of separate signal heads for separate routes was at the East Branch Home Signal, 2 to 9 on the diagram. As this signal allowed a movement into any one of eight different platforms, Nos 3 to 10, it would have been impractical to provide it with that number of separate signal heads. Accordingly an illuminated route indicator was fitted. A similar arrangement was provided on the posts of the down local and down through inner home signals, Nos 71-78 and 89-96 respectively. Likewise, on the West Branch, Inner Home Signal, Nos. 181-183, although here only three platforms are available to trains coming from Hove.

To locomotive crews and motormen used to a straightforward signalling system, albeit accompanied by a veritable forest of semaphore signals as in the past, some of these changes must have appeared substantial, not least because, at a number of signals approaching the platforms at Brighton, the yellow and green aspects could have a variation in meaning. A red indication obviously still meant stop, but the yellow meant 'Proceed, but the platform road was partially occupied by vehicles'. The green indicated that the route was clear to the buffer stops, with the shunt signal used for a light engine when the platform was fully occupied. An exception to this rule was when Nos 78, 96, or 141 was reversed. Each of these allowed a movement into No 4 platform, where it will be seen an additional signal, No 104 was fitted. A yellow signal, displayed as above, had the separate meaning that the line was clear only as far as signal No 104. Whether these complications,

Opposite above - Comparisons at Copyhold Junction. Top is 'U' class No 794 at the head of an Eastbourne express which includes two Pullman cars. The signal box controlling the junction is on the left and was one of those abolished in 1932. To the right is the line to Horstead Keynes.

Below - Some years later at Copyhold Junction, with on the left, the main lines seen heading north. The line from Haywards Heath through Ardingly to Horstead Keynes was electrified in 1935, although passenger services ceased in October 1963. For some time before this, much of the down branch had been used for storage, including in the late 1950s new electric units destined for the Kent Coast scheme. Later condemned wagons were often stabled as far as Horstead Keynes. 'K' Class No 32343 is seen coming off the branch in March 1960 with a working of such stock.

Access to the new signal cabin at Brighton, hardly, perhaps, the most attractive structure ever built, but space constraints were a major consideration, was on foot via a former signal bridge, also used to carry many of the signal cables. Other cables were carried underneath the lines, in a subway provided in 1881 at the time of the station remodelling and formerly used for mechanical rodding and mechanical signal control. (See illustrations on page 76 of SW Issue No 3).

together with the other new initiative of 'wait and proceed', created issues later is not reported. Likewise, there is no evidence to suggest adverse comment from the Board of Trade Inspectorate to the new works at the time. Sand-drags of between 17 and 30 feet in length were provided at the extreme ends of each platform road.

Brighton station area was broken into sections for signalling and operating purposes, using the letters 'A' through to 'F' and approach shunt signals Nos. 31, 32, 99 and 105 were provided. In addition to the function applicable to their name, they also reacted to running movements made past them and were also referred to as 'running shunts'.

Departures from platforms 3 to 10 were made under the control of three aspect signals, having a route indicator able to show 'B' for the Lewes branch or 'T' for the through main line. This was an alternative to the splitting signals used elsewhere and was employed for platform starting signals and at signals where all movements were at a slow speed. Looking back, the whole can be seen as the first steps in a progression towards the colour light signalling we know today.

Due to the curvature of the actual station platforms and consequent visibility problems for train crews, platforms 4, 5, 6 and 7 were provided with repeaters for the starting signals mid way along the platforms. The red indication is again self explanatory, although a yellow or green was accompanied by a further visual display letter of either 'M' or 'S'. Here the letters indicated 'M' for a train destined for the through route or branch and 'S' for a shunt move. One of the

John Webb, referred to on Page 76 of SW Issue 3, has also come to us to recount the names of some of the men working Brighton Box around 1948 together with the sections they would regularly control. These included, Charlie Luff - main and east, 'Chummy' Williams - west, Les Williams - west, Stan Plant - west relief, Jack Roberts - main and east, Bill Scrace - main and east relief, Alf Shoulders - main and east, and Wally Farrington - main and east. In addition there was a Yard Master, Cocker Davies, who at busy periods would work from the box, directing the various shunt movements. In addition to the names of his work colleagues, John has recounted a couple of stories of his time as a 'boy' in the box. At this period the Station Master was renowned for being a good natured and fair man, whilst his assistant was perhaps best described as being of opposite character. One day John answered the phone to hear the assistant SM request to speak to the west side signalman. John responded that man was busy at the time and the caller was politely informed he would be connected as soon as possible. Evidently this was not acceptable to the senior man, as he continued to demand to be put through at once, only to be advised that the signalman was genuinely still occupied. After several requests John admits he lost his temper and not only swore as his superior but also put the phone down. Not surprisingly he was summonsed to a higher authority, although the Station Master let him off with a verbal warning, at the same time seeming to have great difficulty in stopping himself laughing out loud. It was this same station master who was fortunately noticed to be on him way to visit the box one day, when the signalman had one of his colleagues bicycles in pieces in front of the lever frame, attempting to effect a repair. The machine together with parts, spanners and the like were quickly hidden behind the frame, just in time as well - the Station Master never did see them!

Inner platform signal - left, for departing trains on Platform 4. This repeated the indication of Nos 155/156/157. On the right is the 'In' signal for Platform 3.
At Brighton the new works also included lengthening some of the platforms, whilst major rebuilding took place at Haywards Heath.

reasons for this repeated indication, even allowing for the variations in indications and meanings, was to prevent a Guard giving the 'right away' to the driver without being able to clearly observe the indication displayed by the starting signal. The rules have always been clear over this point, in that a train must not be flagged away unless the guard has observed the signal controlling the movement is clear. In more recent years several accidents have occurred, although not at Brighton, where the Guard or station staff, have indicated that a train might proceed. The driver, on receiving this indication, has set off having failed to observe the signal. The phenomenon became known as the 'ding-ding and away we go' scenario. In later years simpler methods of repeating the signal were devised and the familiar small square box, displaying the word 'off' (OFF indicator), or a banner signal were provided ,to assist traffic department staff or the driver, where there were problems with sighting the starting signal.

The Brighton installation called for 51 new colour light running signals and 86 shunt signals. The latter were of the two aspect globe type, having four circular coloured discs for each aspect. This allowed for combinations of colours according to the indication needed – red and green, red and yellow, or yellow and green. 22 route indicators were fitted and 115 electric point machines. The point machines were battery powered, but with the batteries charged through transformer rectifier units, which were fed from a 440v AC supply.

To control the installation a new signal box was constructed at Brighton, on the side of the works building. Whilst certainly modern in both equipment and operation, the much-restricted space in the station area meant it was perhaps hardly the most visually

appealing. This was contemporarily described as 'fire-proof' and displayed the, then new, Southern practice of having its 225 frame of miniature levers facing the rear wall, with the levers divided into three sections: 1-65, 66-125, and 126-225. Basically these were East branch, Main line, and West branch respectively, although there were also obvious *'crossovers'* of operation. In place of the more conventional mechanical interlocking on the levers, electric lever interlocking was provided by the use of normal and reverse lever bands, arranged such that the circuit was only made when the levers were in the correct position.

Two split illuminated diagrams were provided, both set at a slight angle and designed to be visible from any part of the frame, at the same time reducing eye strain for the signalman. A light green colour background to the panel was used, similar to the colour that would become commonplace on a future generation of 'entry-exit' panels. Electric repeaters behind the levers indicated the aspect displayed by the signal or the position of a turnout. Signals that were provided with route indicators also had the route indicator repeated over the lever applicable to the route set.

Train describers for despatching any one of up to for 24 different types of train were provided at the ends and between the sections of the locking frame. These connected with the signal boxes at Brighton Upper Goods, Preston Park, and Hove East. Similar instruments for receiving trains from these locations were located above the frame. Not mentioned in contemporary reports is the means of working to London Road, although it will be noted from one of the photographs that block-bells were in place at that side of the frame, dealing with movements to and from the East branch. This might imply block-bells were still in use at the time the photograph was taken and this could well

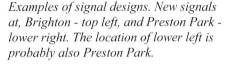

Examples of signal designs. New signals at, Brighton - top left, and Preston Park - lower right. The location of lower left is probably also Preston Park.

Despite the modern developments, things now taken for granted, such as hot axle box detectors and axle box counters, were still some way into the future.

have been the case for a short time, although later it is believed similar train describers were installed.

Between the sections of lever frame were telephones for the use of the signalmen, which mainly communicated with the telephones on the signal posts. Two separate telephone switchboards, manned by 'boys', were positioned between the lever frame and front windows. Calls could also be rerouted from one switchboard to the other as necessary.

A modern feature for the time was the provision of automatically switched lighting inside the box, whenever darkness descended or whenever the ambient light outside was reduced. Thermostatically controlled heating was also provided.

Excluding the displaced mechanical boxes on the main line referred to earlier, the new box at Brighton enabled six mechanical boxes in the Brighton area to be closed, the numbers referring to the number of levers at each location:

Lovers Walk - 60
Brighton North
(also referred to as Montpelier Junction) - 98
Brighton South - 240

Brighton West - 120
New England - 34
Holland Road - 30

The new installation of 225 levers in the power frame now replaced 582 mechanically worked levers.

With the commissioning of the Brighton box, colour light signalling was now provided throughout from Coulsdon North, 14 miles south of Victoria through to the Sussex coast, which represented at the time the greatest length of continuous track circuiting and complete power signalling on a British main line.

Within a very short space of time, notwithstanding the fact that staff had to quickly become familiar with the new equipment, there was also an indication of an improvement in timekeeping. Between 1st and 15th October, the two weeks prior to the conversion, arrivals were an average of 1.1 minute late and departures 0.4 minutes late.

Commencing though with the day of the actual conversion and monitored over the next six days, the results are shown in the table on page 26.

The whole signalling scheme was an essential prelude to the inauguration of the full public electric

Above - starting signals for the Main or East Branch from Platforms 5 and 6. Numbers 153/154 and 150/151. The box at the top displayed the respective route indicator letter. Below are the associated shunt signals.

An interesting comment appeared as a tailpiece in many of the 'yellow' notices:
"OBSERVATION OF TRAINS BY STATION STAFF. Station Staff must, whenever practicable, notice each train as it passes. If they observe anything unusual (such as signals of alarm by a passenger, goods falling off, a vehicle on the lire, a hot axle box . mishap, or a train without a tail lamp or with the tail light out, or a train divided) they must at once telephone the particulars to the next station or signal box. If the circumstances require it, they must arrange for any train on the opposite or parallel line to be stopped.
The Station Master or Signalman receiving the telephone must deal with the emergency as may be found necessary in accordance with the relevant Rules and Regulations. Should there be any reason to believe that the permanent way has been damaged or fouled, trains must not be allowed to proceed until the line has been examined and found to be safe for the passage of trains."
In this respect, the identical same duty performed by the signalman was now diluted.
Right - resumé of signals boxes fully open, open when required, or closed under the new work.

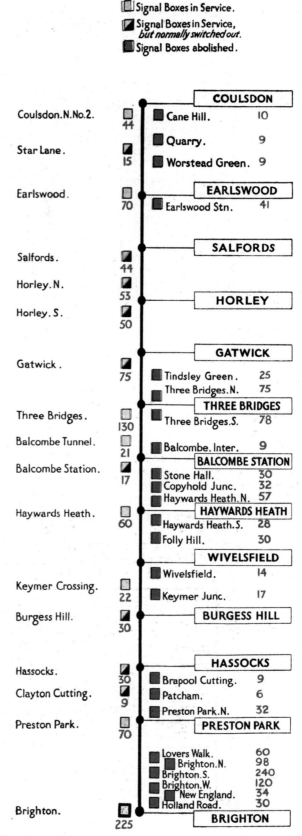

Signal Boxes in Service.
Signal Boxes in Service, *but normally switched out.*
Signal Boxes abolished.

Location		Associated box	Number
		COULSDON	
Coulsdon.N.No.2.	44	Cane Hill.	10
Star Lane.	15	Quarry.	9
		Worstead Green.	9
Earlswood.	70	**EARLSWOOD**	
		Earlswood Stn.	41
Salfords.	44	**SALFORDS**	
Horley.N.	53		
Horley.S.	50	**HORLEY**	
Gatwick.	75	**GATWICK**	
		Tindsley Green.	25
		Three Bridges.N.	75
Three Bridges.	130	**THREE BRIDGES**	
		Three Bridges.S.	78
Balcombe Tunnel.	21	Balcombe. Inter.	9
Balcombe Station.	17	**BALCOMBE STATION**	
		Stone Hall.	30
		Copyhold Junc.	32
		Haywards Heath.N.	57
Haywards Heath.	60	**HAYWARDS HEATH**	
		Haywards Heath.S.	28
		Folly Hill.	30
		WIVELSFIELD	
		Wivelsfield.	14
Keymer Crossing.	22	Keymer Junc.	17
Burgess Hill.	30	**BURGESS HILL**	
Hassocks.	30	**HASSOCKS**	
		Brapool Cutting.	9
Clayton Cutting.	9	Patcham.	6
		Preston Park.N.	32
Preston Park.	70	**PRESTON PARK**	
		Lovers Walk.	60
		Brighton.N.	98
		Brighton.S.	240
		Brighton.W.	120
		New England.	34
		Holland Road.	30
Brighton.	225	**BRIGHTON**	

service on the route between Victoria and Brighton / Hove and Worthing, which commenced on 1st January 1933.

Further evidence that both the electric service and with it the revised signalling was a success can be gauged from the two quotes which follow.

"On Whit-Monday, 1933, 107 trains left Brighton in five hours, carrying 75,000 passengers

In the course of the homeward rush from the seaside on Monday evening last, there were several achievements on the part of the Southern Railway calling for attention. At Brighton a special control tower was installed and brought into use about 4 p.m., its object being to direct passengers to the various platforms and trains. Between 5 p.m. and 10 p.m. no fewer than 107 trains left Brighton Central Station, carrying 75,000 passengers. On the average, therefore, a train departed every three minutes - or slightly less - throughout the five hour period, and each train carried on an average just over 700 passengers -15,000 an hour. The great bulk of this traffic was for London or beyond, and had to be carried over the main line, which has only the one up track as far as Balcombe Tunnel box - 19 miles - and in addition to the trains from Brighton there were those from Worthing and Hove also passing over almost the whole of this distance. More noteworthy still is the fact that from Keymer Junction to Balcombe Tunnel there were also the Hastings, Bexhill, Eastbourne and Seaford trains to be accommodated by the single up road in addition to those from Brighton and Worthing. Actually, between Keymer Junction and Haywards Heath the up trains moving over this road were between 7 and 8 p.m., 13 trains; between 8 and 9 p.m., 16; between 9 and 10 p.m., 18; and between 10 and 11 p.m., 14 trains, the greatest density being one every 3.3 minutes throughout the hour, Only by the employment of automatic colour-light signalling, and of very heavy electric trains* for the most part, could this traffic be moved within so short a period".

* the reference should probably read "an intensive electric train service".

Reprinted from "Railway Gazette" June 9th, 1933

"The combination of good weather and improved traveling facilities resulted in a great increase of passenger traffic on the Southern Railway during the Whitsun recess. During the whole holiday period no less than 129,165 passengers were conveyed to Brighton, mainly by electric trains. This represents an increase of 75 per cent, over last year. On Whit-Sunday the number of people carried to Brighton showed an increase of 174 per cent, over last Whit-Sunday, while on Whit-Monday the increase was 68 per cent".

Reprinted from "Modern Transport," June 10th, 1933

Acknowledgements: The genus for this article was the loan of several 'Yellow Notices' from the collection of Colin Hall and formerly belonging William Hall, a Southern Railway Motorman. (See 'Southern Way No 1 – September 2007, pages 34/35). This was followed by the acquisition of the 'Supplement to the Railway Gazette' for 30th December 1932, dealing specifically with the extension of electrification on the Brighton line. Next, Signalling Engineer Irvine Cresswell arrived with the loan of several publicity booklets from signalling manufacturers, including that from Westinghouse

Table Showing Average Minutes Late - 1933			
		Arrivals	**Departures**
Sunday	16th October	8.4	9.0
Monday	17th October	8.5	10.6
Tuesday	18th October	2.5	3.1
Wednesday	19th October	3.0	1.9
Thursday	20th October	1.6	1.0
Friday	21st October	0.7	0.3

dealing with the Brighton Line. This was followed by retired Signalling Engineer Tony Goodyear, with his experience of SR signalling and procedures. Both Irvine and Tony have read the text and commented thereon. Finally, former railwayman John Webb, a booking-lad at Brighton power box in early BR days, has added his own memories of working. Gentleman, many thanks to you all.

Tony Goodyear has agreed to commence planning for a major series of articles on the SR to appear in 'Southern Way' in future issues. These will look at the Southern from a new perspective, and commencing with the contributions brought to the new regime by the constituent companies allied to their own strengths and weaknesses. The whole promises to be a fascinating viewpoint and we look forward to having the first in print in the near future.

References:

Southern Electric 1909 – 1968, G T Moody, Published Ian Allan, pages 28 and 48

Understandably Messrs Westinghouse were keen to record and publicise their involvement, but they also took a number of views of the old system as well. Here, as an example, 'King Arthur' class No 802 'Sir Dunmore' waits at the end of the platform at Brighton ready for departure. In the background is the mechanical 'West' box, which contained 120 levers.

Kidderminster Railway Museum / Westinghouse collection 057040.

THE LEGACY OF Mr PRICE

On 5th September 1921, near to Haywards Heath, a fatal accident occurred, the only casualty being Mr Price, a passenger. We have no details as to the service involved, although we do know that "A portion of the engine step broke away and flew through the carriage window striking Mr Price on the head". Whether this was from the engine hauling the train pulling Mr Price's carriage, or a passing train is not known. The photographs are a set of four from an album purchased at auction in 2007 and known to have come from the archive of the late R C 'Dick Riley. In appearance the actual album would seem to be one compiled by the LBSCR as there are file references included to this incident. With due respect to the deceased, the tragedy did mean the recording of the interior of an LBSCR compartment of the period, something rarely seen and for that we must be grateful. Curiously, the view of the engine step on the next page, seems to be complete and no obvious broken section can be discerned. The views have been shown to John Minnis, who kindly comments that the LBSCR were well known for what were believed to be enamelled iron adverts on the doors of third class stock.

From the builders plate it is possible to identify the locomotive as 'I3' No 79, built at Brighton in 1910. It would survive in service under British Railways until November 1950.

All 27 of the 'I3's survived into BR days, although by this period their condition was far from that seen above. As a fireman at Brighton, prior to his transfer to the Traffic Department, John Webb recalled an occasion with one of the class, which he subsequently discovered had been in store for some time previously. John and his driver took over the engine, the number was not reported, at Brighton station and on checking it was noticed the pressure gauge was right on maximum. Expecting the engine to blow off at any moment the injector was put on, although this had no effect on the gauge. It remained in this fashion for some time and so the crew took the engine to shed thinking the gauge was faulty. There the fitters isolated the supply and inserted their master gauge. On reconnecting the steam supply, however, the pressure shown was in excess of 300 psi, this was against the normal maximum working pressure of just 180 psi. The engine was quickly moved as far away from the shed as possible and the fire blacked in to allow it to cool. Fortunately all was well, although a subsequent check of the safety valves showed them to be rusted solid, the effect of having been stored for some time. Not surprisingly, the engine never worked again, although it remained notionally 'on-stock' until withdrawn some months later.

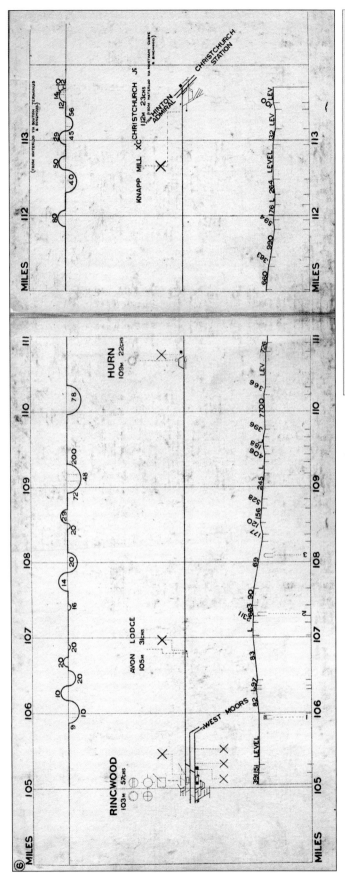

AVON LODGE SIDING

The points leading to and from this Siding, which is situated on the Up side of the Line about 1½ miles from Ringwood, are operated from a ground frame, and controlled by the tablet for the Ringwood West and Hurn section, in accordance with the regulation for controlling Sidings by means of the Electric Train Tablet.

A gate, which must be kept across the Siding except when wagons are being worked to or from the Siding, is provided at the Company's boundary.

The key of the gate is held by the Gateman at Avon Lodge.

Down Goods Trains perform work at the Siding, and the Gateman at Avon Lodge Crossing will attend to each Train required to do work at the Siding.

The siding is on a gradient of 1 in 83 falling towards Ringwood.

(LSWR Appendix to Book of Rules and Regulations and to the Working Timetables, 25th July 1921. Items in italics were omitted from the similar, but earlier Appendix dated 1st January 1911).

Opposite page - a remarkable view of Hurn looking towards Christchurch, which whilst undated is probably from around 1900. Whilst today Hurn (several variations in the spelling have appeared in timetables over the years including Hurne, Herne and Hearne), now a suburb of Bournemouth, at the time the location was distinctly rural and dependant upon its agricultural community, as witness the churns on the up platform. The signal box is of typical South Western style and was the only intermediate block-post between Ringwood and Christchurch. Indeed, here at Hurn was the only passing loop. Beyond the up platform was a loading dock, whilst on the up side, but at the north end of the station, was a single goods siding. A ground frame controlled the points at the north end of the loop.

John Allsop Collection

Left - extract from the LSWR system maps of gradients and curves Circa 1914.

From RINGWOOD to CHRISTCHURCH
an almost forgotten railway

Of all the routes of the former LSWR, that from Ringwood through Hurn to Christchurch and Bournemouth must be one of the most obscure and least illustrated. Originally part of the first line to reach Bournemouth from the east, its importance took an immediate decline, following the opening of the direct connection from Brockenhurst, through Sway to Christchurch, in 1888.

To be fair, traffic had never perhaps been to the level expected and the original single line would remain with just one passing loop at Hurn. A casualty under the harsh economic times of the 1930s, the route was closed completely by the Southern Railway on 30th September 1935, the same date as the closure of the Lynton and Barnstaple line.

Prior to 2007 the history of the route had been sadly neglected, although this has now been addressed in Vol 1 of the 'Castlemans's Corkscrew', dealing with the Nineteenth Century by Brian Jackson, published by Oakwood Press. (Part 2 should be available in late 2008.)

Despite what is excellent historical account now being available, photographic coverage of the line is still weak and consequently we are delighted to be able to present this medley of views.

Left and above - The even more obscure stopping place at Avon Lodge north of Hurn, provided, it is believed, from the time of opening of the line in 1862. Intended to serve the estate of Lord Malmesbury, the stopping place was provided partly in recompense for allowing the railway to be built through 22 acres of the 1,000 acre estate. (Other reports refer to an estate having in excess of 1,300 acres.) The railway had also to provide four level crossings and a lodge and siding at Avon Lodge with the occupier of the cottage having the right to stop any ordinary passenger train to pick up and set down passengers. How much this right was exercised over the years is not known. Nearby Avon Castle was reputed to have been built in 1878, some years after the railway and stopping place had been opened, at a cost of £80,000. It is possible that in 1862, Avon Lodge was seen solely as a convenient railhead for goods for the estate. In 1912 the 10th Earl of Egremont purchased Avon Castle and continued to reside there until he succumbed to injuries received in a motoring accident in 1932. The new Earl, formerly Mr F J Percival, inherited the estate from his late cousin although it was subsequently broken up with Avon Castle itself becoming luxury flats, several private houses being erected in the grounds. The photograph on the left was purportedly taken circa 1932, at the time when a new succession was taking place. How much, if any use of the railway here was made by the Earl is unclear, Presumably the gatekeeper (crossing-keeper), was an employee of the railway, a railway cottage being provided as seen above. It may well be that the adjacent waiting room, seen behind the two seated men, saw little use.

Passengers wishing to alight at Avon Lodge would advise the guard beforehand whilst for those wishing to join distant signals were provided in either direction and worked from the crossing keepers hut. These were normally kept in the 'off' position, but returned to 'on' as an indication to the driver that a stop was required.

In the left hand view an 'up' Ringwood bound train has paused at the station. The railway employee is possibly the guard. Was he even waiting for the photographer to rejoin the service? It is possible to confirm that push-pull working was in operation on the line at this time. Just visible under the coach is a fouling bar and the FPL for the single goods siding, which was located on the west side of the line.

With thanks to John Allsop, Nick Catford, Colin Chivers, Richard Foxwell,
Keith Hastie, and Dennis Tillman in the preparation of this article. The signalling and track
diagrams are reproduced from the respective volumes of George Pryer and A V Paul.

SNAPSHOTS OF HURN

As a means of economy, the passing loop at Hurn was taken out of use from 9ᵗʰ August 1927 and presumably removed shortly afterwards. The signal box was also reduced in status to a ground frame, with the single line section now operating throughout between Ringwood and Christchurch. The former ground frame at the north end of the site was also abolished at the same time. Due to the presence of the level crossing, stop signals were retained in either direction.
The siding was retained although, as before, it is likely goods traffic was limited.

As seen from the previous page, traffic was by now restricted to push-pull workings operating as a shuttle between Ringwood and Bournemouth.

Centre right, the staff, a porter and platelayers, would appear to be using a trolley to move domestic furniture, it being possible to identify at least two chairs and a roll of carpet.

Following closure, the track was lifted in July 1937, whilst the former station site has for some years been known as the Avon Causeway Hotel which follows a general railway theme.

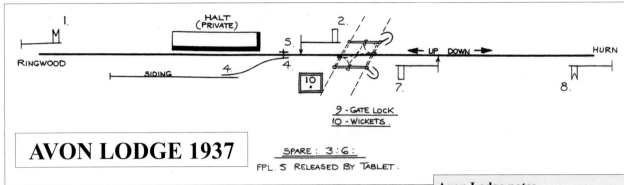

AVON LODGE HALT - 1920

C ⟶ GF
LC
HALT (PRIVATE)
105. 34
To Ringwood
(SEE ROUTE 51/01)
C

AVON LODGE 1937

HALT (PRIVATE)

RINGWOOD
1.
M
SIDING
4.
5.
4.
2.
10.
← UP DOWN →
7.
8.
HURN

9 - GATE LOCK
10 - WICKETS.

SPARE : 3 : 6 :
FPL. 5 RELEASED BY TABLET.

Avon Lodge notes

NOT A BLOCK POST.
GROUND-LEVEL BUILDING - TYPE UNCONFIRMED.
TYPE OF LEVER FRAME NOT KNOWN.
FPL STANDS NORMALLY "IN" AND IS RELEASED
BY HURN - RINGWOOD WEST TABLET.

NOTE: BOX NOT MANNED FOR ENTIRE TRAIN SERVICE, BUT
ONLY FOR HOURS AS ARRANGED BY TRAFFIC SUPERINTENDANT.
AT OTHER TIMES CROSSING OPERATED BY TRAIN CREWS.

SECTION OF LINE CLOSED 30-09-1935 AND BOX CLOSED

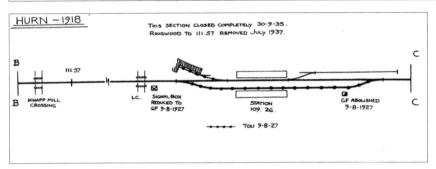

HURN - 1918

THIS SECTION CLOSED COMPLETELY 30-9-35.
RINGWOOD TO 111.57 REMOVED JULY 1937.

B
111.57
KNAPP MILL CROSSING
LC
SIGNAL BOX REDUCED TO GF 9-8-1927
STATION 109. 26.
GF ABOLISHED 9-8-1927
C
C

•–•–•– TOU 9-8-27

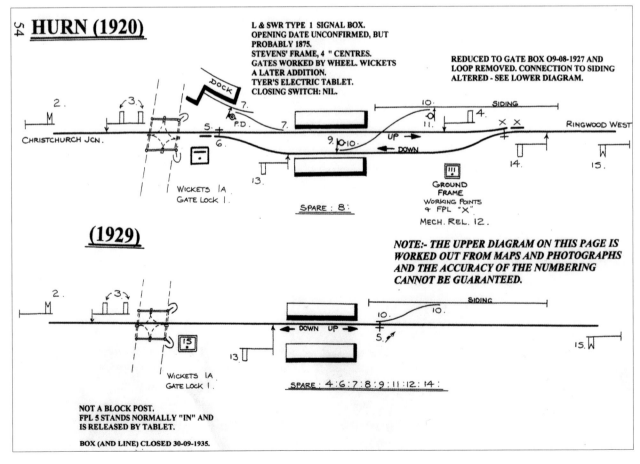

54 **HURN (1920)**

L & SWR TYPE 1 SIGNAL BOX.
OPENING DATE UNCONFIRMED, BUT
PROBABLY 1875.
STEVENS' FRAME, 4 " CENTRES.
GATES WORKED BY WHEEL. WICKETS
A LATER ADDITION.
TYER'S ELECTRIC TABLET.
CLOSING SWITCH: NIL.

REDUCED TO GATE BOX 09-08-1927 AND
LOOP REMOVED. CONNECTION TO SIDING
ALTERED - SEE LOWER DIAGRAM.

DOCK
2.
M
3.
7.
P.D.
5.
6.
7.
9. 10
13.
10.
11.
SIDING
4.
× ×
UP →
← DOWN
14.
15.
RINGWOOD WEST

CHRISTCHURCH JCN.

WICKETS 1A
GATE LOCK 1.

GROUND FRAME
WORKING POINTS
& FPL "X"
MECH. REL. 12.

SPARE : 8 :

(1929)

NOTE:- THE UPPER DIAGRAM ON THIS PAGE IS
WORKED OUT FROM MAPS AND PHOTOGRAPHS
AND THE ACCURACY OF THE NUMBERING
CANNOT BE GUARANTEED.

2.
M
3.
15
13.
← DOWN UP →
5.
10.
10.
SIDING
15. W

WICKETS 1A
GATE LOCK 1.

SPARE : 4 : 6 : 7 : 8 : 9 : 11 : 12 : 14 :

NOT A BLOCK POST.
FPL 5 STANDS NORMALLY "IN" AND
IS RELEASED BY TABLET.

BOX (AND LINE) CLOSED 30-09-1935.

Understandably train services, on what was in effect little more than a rural branch line, are known to have been limited. Indeed for many years, when this was still the only means of accessing Bournemouth from the east, the line being extended from Christchurch to Bournemouth in 1870, there were just three services in either direction.

Despite the opening of the direct route to Bournemouth in 1888, by the summer of 1901 the number of trains had increased and were operating to the rather interesting timetable below. All Down trains commenced from Ringwood and there was no Sunday service.

A similar service was operating by 1909, although there were also now two services on Sunday, both shown as worked by rail-motor.

By 1914 an evening service was shown, running from Ringwood only as far as Hurn where it reversed and returned to Ringwood. Five years later, in 1919, a deterioration had set in, with a rather shabby three trains each way on weekdays only, all running just between Bournemouth Central and Ringwood. The journey time had also increased being 22 minutes at best and 25 minutes at worst. The Sunday service had also been withdrawn.

What is not clear is whether following the completion of the Bournemouth Direct line and the continuation of the line westwards from that point (the former Bournemouth East Station) in 1888, the line through Hurn was ever used for relief or excursion services.

Apart from reference in the 1901 book to the Goods service running when required and one occasion in the 1909 timetable when there is mention of Avon Lodge being serviced from Ringwood, 'as required', there is no mention of any regular goods working. This may indicate that mixed trains were operated at some stage during the early years, although later the operation of motor workings meant a locomotive was probably despatched as necessary. With milk and parcels probably handled by passenger services, it was probably just coal or agricultural produce that would demand any form of special working.

1901 - DOWN	am	am	am	pm	pm	pm	pm,
Ringwood: dep	08.00		10.45	12.00	3.48	6.45	10.03
Avon Lodge:	Q		Q	Q	Q	Q	Q
Hurn: arr	08.12		10.57	12.12	4.02	6.56	10.15
Hurn: dep	08.13	09.05	10.58	12.13	4.03	6.57	10.16
Christchurch: arr	08.19	09.12	11.04	12.18	4.08	7.02	10.22
Note	1	2	1	3	3	4	5

(1) To Bournemouth West and then Wimborne. (2) Goods, runs when required. (3) To Swanage. (4) To Bournemouth West. (5) To Bournemouth Central. Except as shown all trains terminate at Ringwood. No Sunday service.

1901 - UP	am	am	am	am	pm	pm	pm,	pm
Christchurch: dep	06.57	08.45	09.47	11.15	3.17	5.58	8.43	11.13
Hurn: arr	07.02	08.52	09.52	11.21	3.23	6.02	8.48	11.18
Hurn: dep	07.03		09.53	11.22	3.24	6.04	8.49	11.19
Avon Lodge:	Q		Q	Q	Q	Q	Q	Q
Ringwood: arr	07.14		10.04	11.34	3.36	6.16	9.01	11.30
Note	1	2	3	4	3	5	6	7

(1) From Bournemouth Central. (2) Shown as goods although not with a 'runs as required' note. (3) From Bournemouth West. (4) From Swanage. (5) From Salisbury via Bournemouth West. After arrival at Ringwood shown as non-stop to Waterloo arriving at 9.51 pm. (6) First appears in the timetable at Hamworthy Junction with no indication of an original starting point. Thursdays only from Bournemouth Central.

Peter Bailey has kindly read this article and raises a number of issues which we cannot answer, but perhaps someone else can. First the obvious, the stock workings to enable the services in the tables to be operated beggar belief. Does anyone have an LSWR carriage working book for the period?
Down service No 1. Did it become a Wimborne - Ringwood local to return the train to its starting place?
Up service No 5. Was there, seriously, a continuous working, Salisbury - Verwood - Wimborne - Bournemouth West - Bournemouth Central - Ringwood - Waterloo?
The whole appears to indicate that the branch services were in fact parts of considerably longer journeys.

Further information would be welcomed.

RAY CHORLEY

Our recollections of Ray – a Gentleman amongst the back-room boys. Born 13th August 1932, lost to the hobby, 5th November 2007.

Ray was born in Plymouth and then lived in the Devon village of Brixham, until his father's work with Trinity House, took the family to Sussex. After finishing schooling, he became a Southern Railway craft apprentice at Lancing Works. An interruption for National Service saw Ray serving in the RAF, with postings to Hornchurch, Cardington, Kirkham (Blackpool) and finally Boscombe Down. It was whilst at Cardington, on a weapons and explosives course, that Ray formed a lifelong friendship with Benson Chamley. Ray would often stay with Ben in Yorkshire, enjoying walking and pot-holing.

Returning to Lancing, Ray later moved into the drawing office, a move of which he was justifiably proud and which was also to set the seal upon his career. Starting as a junior draughtsman, he steadily progressed up the grades and was transferred to Eastleigh in the early 1960s. It was here, in 1965, that he joined the then Mid Hants Model Railway Group, a small, but highly professional society and where membership was, "by invitation". For the time, their 00 layout was to a very high standard and, when exhibiting, all members were similarly attired and wore identical white jackets. I belonged to the sister club in Poole and we held joint exhibitions in both towns. As a teenager I had never before seen this level of modelling or professionalism.

Whilst at Eastleigh works and no doubt due to his own interests, Ray was designated to deal with the many requests originating from modellers et al. No doubt because of his own enthusiasm, the enquirers often received more than they had bargained for! It was likewise whilst in this post, that he met Alan Blackburn and Gerry Bixley, forming not just a professional, but also a lasting personal friendship. His first contribution to the wider model world began in 1965, with a series of carriage and wagon drawings in 'Model Railway Constructor'.

Mid Hants layout "Mk II", (see 'Railway Modeller' January – May 1974), was now under construction and used many novel ideas, several of which Ray had a hand in; in fact it was Ray who built and tested the first geodetic plywood baseboard, an idea resulting from one of the regular brain-storming sessions with the Group's President, the late Wing-Commander Ken Burns.

Now settled in Hampshire with his wife Margaret and sons Simon and Colin and professionally busy with full-size EMU rolling stock design, a major upheaval occurred with the transfer of BR's design offices to Derby. What were considered to be obsolete drawings were to be consigned to the bonfire and, but

for Ray, would have gone up in smoke, lost for ever. With the blessing of senior management and in his own time, Ray sorted and saved several hundred of these irreplaceable items, many leaving the works in the boot of his trusty Austin Seven. Before he died, these drawings were donated to the HMRS at Butterley. Further, he was later instrumental in helping Bob Essery save many more drawings, this time from the Derby drawing office.

Moving with his family to Whatstandwell, Derbyshire, in the late 1960s, was a major wrench and although not near his old friends, he came to love the area. Sadly Margaret died shortly after this move. He continued his work, being part of the team producing the series of four volumes on SR wagons, without doubt the most comprehensive coverage there is ever likely to be on the subject. Ray personally completed all the drawings for the final volume before becoming seriously ill with cancer. The last drawings were produced on the CAD system, today quite normal, but Ray was a pioneer in the field, as a result of BR sending him to California to study what was then a novel system in order that it might be introduced at Derby. Little did they know to what use Ray would put his new-found knowledge!

I had not seen Ray for many years and he seemed to have lost his enthusiasm for life. By good fortune, he was persuaded to come to one of the Gauge O Guild exhibitions at Telford and was dragged around to see all his old friends, including me. He looked quite unwell and had obviously not taken care of himself for some years. I was only able to recognize him by his very distinctive voice, so familiar over the telephone. One year later he reappeared and again I did not recognize him. He had put on weight, cut his long grey hair, looked very smart and likewise years younger. When asked for his prescription, he answered simply, "June, my wife".

Now retired, Ray and June moved to Crichthey, bought a bed and breakfast business and was thriving, this despite he and June being as different as chalk and cheese. I was given his 'B & B' card and told to come and stay whenever I was in the area. This transpired to be a most convenient arrangement, as when attending the GOG summer show at Halifax, Crich was a marvellous half way house.

Over the next few years I would stay for a week at a time and we covered a couple of thousand miles visiting all the surrounding museums and preserved railways. Ray was in his element, justifiably proud of the rolling stock his team had improved or developed. He was especially pleased with the solution to the 'Whale', the BR version of the SR bogie ballast wagon, which had become notorious as it sometimes only managed one loaded journey between repairs. Ray

QUESTIONS, QUESTIONS....?

Above - A good friend to 'Southern Way' is Dennis Callender, who was active as a photographer recording the Southern scene in the early 1950s. Amongst Dennis's views is this tantalising scene of a westbound train passing Millbrook. No date unfortunately. But look at the last two vehicles. One, at least, a 6-wheel coach yet evidently still in service and displaying an 'M' suffix to its number. (The actual print has been included to maximum size at the bottom whilst the number may well be similar to M21015.) Many questions, and only supposition to assist at this stage. The only clue so far is that it could be a Fawley line service, but again why the double heading? Unless the 6-wheelers were being transferred for internal use at either Marchwood or Fawley - hence the second loco as well. We could be hopelessly off-track of course so any ideas would be most welcome.

Left - Another puzzler from Dennis. The location is clearly Exeter Central, but why the second 'Pacific' at the rear? (Sorry no definite loco identity either.) Is the fact that there is an awful lot of steam around a clue, meaning a loco failure? But if so why the second engine at the rear, unless this was to pull the stock clear? Perhaps someone with a profound knowledge of the workings at Exeter will say that this was a regular practice. Well, we only asked!

took a ride on one, returned to the office and designed some new plates thereby solving the problem. Amongst other stock, he designed the 'Seacow' and 'Sealion' hoppers, whilst he was also responsible for designing a nuclear flask wagon.

In the summer of 2007, I again stayed with Ray for what would be the last time. His health had deteriorated and although he came with me on two or three trips he was visibly weak. He and June had also decided to live in Spain rather than as previous, visit for a few months each year. The B & B was thus sold and in the autumn they moved their new home. Sadly Ray deteriorated suddenly and after a few weeks in a distressingly dark tunnel he came to rest at the terminus of life.

Over the years, many model manufacturers

and modellers alike have been grateful for his assistance; from the large such as Airfix / GMR and Slater's to others such as Roxey and myself at ABS. Not many people knew about the help that he so quickly offered and he would never ask for anything in return. He was one of the few who was aware that precise information and accurate drawings are the key to producing good models and he actually did something about it. His work will be remembered and valued, as long as there is as interest in modelling the Southern.

Our sympathies go to his wife June, his sons Colin and Simon, and step brother Peter and their families. My thanks also to Gerry Bixley, Alan Blackburn, Douglas Hewitt and David Yule in compiling these notes. **Adrian B Swain**

BRITISH RAILWAYS – SOUTHERN REGION MAGAZINE

Jeffery Grayer reviews the second and what was to prove to be final volume of this short-lived publication, which appeared for the last time in December 1949, before being absorbed into the new "British Railways Magazine".

In 1881 three young clerks of the South Western Railway, including a certain Sam Fay later to become Sir Sam Fay, Superintendent of the LSWR and latterly General Manager of the MSWJR and of the Great Central, produced the first number of the "*South Western Gazette*", a newspaper for the staff, by the staff. This periodical lasted until January 1923 when, following grouping, the title changed to the "*Southern Railway Magazine*" which was to continue for 25 years, encompassing not only the former South Western but also the LBSC and SER sections. The monthly print run was 20,000 copies selling at 3d a time. It continued uninterrupted throughout the Second World War, although restricted to a bi-monthly appearance with pages reduced from 40 to 16. Following nationalisation the title changed to the "*Southern Region Magazine*", but this was to last just two years, until the end of 1949 when the Railway Executive decided to appoint full time staff to produce a "*British Railways Magazine*".

A review of the final volume, the 12 issues for 1949 reveals some significant and fascinating events, some of the most interesting and quirky of which are detailed below.

JANUARY

Sir Eustace Missenden OBE, Chairman of the Railway Executive, in giving a New Year message to all 658,000 BR staff (a staggering figure in comparison to today's railway industry), summarised the first year of the newly nationalised industry by stating that, "*The stage in economic progress of the country, and the continued rise in cost of everything we have to pay for, the fall in public spending power, and the shortages of essential materials – notably steel – have hampered our efforts during the past twelve months. Traffics have fallen , while we have not been able to go nearly as fast as we would like with the replacement of worn-out carriages, nor with schemes for improving both public and staff amenities. Despite fewer coaches we have contrived to provide the public with the best summer and winter train services since before the war, and our freight services are being progressively accelerated and improved*". He concluded by re-affirming the objectives, "*which I am sure we all have at heart, namely, by zealous service and constant courtesy to enhance the reputation of our calling in the eyes of the public whom we serve*".

Sir Eustace Missenden, O.B.E.

The first in the third series of the Merchant Navy class, "New Zealand Line", was named in a ceremony held at Waterloo on 24th November 1948 attended by H S Whitehouse, Chairman of the New Zealand Shipping Co. Ltd., John Elliot and O V S Bulleid of the Southern Region and the High Commissioner for New Zealand.

A picture of "Loading cyder at Whimple" was accompanied by a note from a local correspondent signing himself "Cider Lad" stating that although the war had interrupted exports of Devon cider it was once again being sent to all parts of the world including Bahrain, Singapore, Trinidad, the Persian Gulf, Egypt and South America, travelling from Whimple to London

or Liverpool Docks for shipment.

In "Reminiscence Corner" a correspondent recalled that " *55 years ago an event took place at the Devils Dyke, Sussex, which was decidedly unusual. This was a balloon ascent from the punchbowl on a Saturday afternoon and 3 - 4,000 passengers were conveyed from Brighton and West Brighton* (latterly Hove) *stations by special trains requiring two 0-4-4 tank engines to surmount the up gradient and curves, no ordinary achievement then for the LBSCR with trains packed to capacity.*" He then went on to recall that "*ten years ago I found myself the only passenger to alight from an ordinary scheduled train for the same terminus.*" (The Dyke branch had closed on 1 January 1939).

To demonstrate that locomotive preservation proposals are nothing new there was considerable correspondence regarding which types of locomotive should be considered as candidates for preservation. Following the announcement made the previous year, which had earmarked an Adams 4-4-0 and a Stroudley Terrier for preservation, it was felt an SECR representative in the form of a Stirling F1 4-4-0 should be added to the list, a suggestion that was endorsed by one correspondent who stated that there were still four examples in service and that if "*I were lucky at Littlewoods, I would offer to buy one myself.*" Other suggestions included a Stirling Goods of Class O, there was apparently an immobile example A98 based at Ramsgate for carriage heating, a Wainwright D Class 4-4-0 and a Stroudley D 0-4-2 tank.

On a more sombre note, it was reported that a ceremony took place at Dover Marine station on 16th December 1948 to mark the return of the first of the French War Dead to their native land for re-interment. The remains had been exhumed at various locations throughout the UK and conveyed to North Camp goods station for forwarding to Dover whence they were shipped on the BR ferry steamer to Dunkerque.

FEBRUARY

The letters page revealed a letter from none other than Sir Herbert Walker, General Manger of the LSWR and SR from 1912 – 1937 saying that, "*You may like to hear of the following fine job of work by some of your people. As you know I came down by the 3.28 pm from Victoria yesterday. We arrived at 4.38 – 3 minutes before the advertised time. At 5.45 I rang up the Stationmaster's Office at Brighton to say I had left my umbrella on the train. At 6.30 pm they rang me up to say the umbrella had been found at London Bridge. I think this beats the record.*"

The Southern Region salvaged 803 tons of waste paper in 1948, reaching their target of contributing one thousandth part of the national figure of 800,000 tons called for by the Board of Trade.

The Chief Medical Officer, Southern Region, produced one of his ongoing series of helpful articles, this time on the fascinating subject of "*Chilblains – Their prevention and cure.*"

A regular punctuality feature of the magazine gave the latest details of timekeeping, for November 1948, in comparison to previous years –

Average Minutes late Arrival (Weekdays)

	Dec 1945	Nov 1946	Nov 1947	Nov 1948
Steam	8.06	2.36	2.23	1.55
Electric	4.97	1.93	2.42	2.09

MARCH

The lead story in this month's issue concerned the naming of 34090 "Sir Eustace Missenden – Southern Railway" at a ceremony held at Waterloo on February 15. Apart from the usual dignitaries, there was a guard of honour specially chosen from amongst the 67,000 SR workers who had given long hours of service during the war including two George Medallists, an OBE and three BEMs, together with two retired railwaymen from

Missenden House, the home for aged SR employees. Sir John Elliot said that *"of all the "Battle of Britain" naming ceremonies that had taken place none was more appropriate than the one they were attending today."* In paying tribute to the men of the SR, Missenden said that *"this locomotive will bear my name but may I say, in all sincerity, that I regard this as only a symbol."* An editor's note mentioned the fact that there were 42 engines in the Battle of Britain class and three more were to be added.

New types of rails of the "flat bottomed", rather than "bull head" type were to become the new standard rail for BR being attached to sleepers by simpler fastening arrangements, making them easier to maintain. The new rails would be of two types – 109lb/yard and 98lb/yard – their use being determined by the nature and speed of the traffic they had to carry.

A further naming ceremony covered this month featured 35022 and 35023 which were named in a joint ceremony at Southampton Docks Berth 101. Whilst on the subject of the docks, it was reported that a new terminal, primarily for ships on the Union Castle line's South African run, was to be erected on the site of No. 102 shed which was destroyed by enemy action.

A champion bull "Creathorne Hero" was pictured arriving at Bude station, prior to his departure for South America, having been sold for stud purposes.

APRIL

The fiftieth anniversary of the Night Ferry was celebrated in this issue with the 500th journey, since its reinstatement on 15th December 1947 after its war time break, being achieved on 28th April 1949. Many distinguished passengers still used this service back in the 1940s including royalty, British and foreign statesmen, international sportsmen, film stars and celebrities. In May 1948 Princess Elizabeth and the Duke of Edinburgh travelled by the service to Paris where they spent a short holiday and later in the summer athletes of many nations used it to attend the Olympic Games at Wembley. Other recent notable travellers included the Duke of Windsor, King Feisal of Iraq and ex-King Michael of Rumania. (The service clung to life throughout the 1970s to finish in October 1980, a travesty of its once premium image).

A new type of public address equipment using plug-in microphones was being widely used on Southern Region stations, Holborn Viaduct, Ramsgate, Margate, Eastbourne, New Cross Gate and Gillingham (Kent) already having been equipped. The microphone can be carried in the pocket and plugged in at sockets provided at suitable points on walls of station buildings or lamp standards. They can be used quite freely in the midst of station noise without the need for special enclosures and

A short
read before sleep.

She's off! The Night Ferry
leaves Victoria.

The head-board
on the French locomotive.

a special locking device prevents any cross-talking, should two microphones be plugged in simultaneously.

The cartoon featured in this month's issue shows that overcrowding was nothing new !!

"It's disgusting, herding us like ordinary passengers."

MAY

A new horse organisation, dealing with the purchase, care and maintenance of the BR stud of (a somewhat amazing) 7,500 horses had recently been brought into operation. The country, split into four territories, were each under the charge of a Horse Superintendent responsible to a Chief Horse Superintendent into whose hands the buying of "motive power" has been concentrated. The working stables remained under Regional control but the stud depots and hospitals were controlled by the new Horse Superintendents. The article concluded by stating that BR horses were gradually being replaced by mechanical transport. (The last horse – Charlie – was not retired from Newmarket until 1967).

An interesting old photograph, entitled "Those Were The days", showed a tea party in progress in the

"The Nation's chin-up Boy" goes west:

Cheerful Charlie Chester and his wife leading Waterloo for the USA on April 6th.

High Street at Okehampton, to celebrate the coming of the railway in 1871 to Okehampton Road (Sampford Courtenay). Meals were apparently served in relays with some school children shown tucking in to the spread.

JUNE

Passengers joining the 0935 Newhaven – Dieppe Boat Train at Victoria on Sunday morning 15th May found electric rather than steam motive power at the head of the train in the shape of 20003, one of the Southern Region's new electric locomotives. This was the first time that a boat train had been worked by an electric engine. This was the third of the class of three, the first two having done sterling work on goods services. They could haul trains at speeds up to 75mph and can be used continuously for several days and nights without maintenance.

The Supporters Club of Faversham Town FC, "The Lillywhites", wrote in to express their appreciation of the service provided by the SR in arranging at least five football specials in the current season, the tie with neighbouring Canterbury attracting over 400 supporters.

Another naming ceremony was reported, this time for 35024 "East Asiatic Company", when Prince Axel of Denmark, the Chairman of the Danish shipping company, performed the honours. 35024 was recorded as being the first SR engine to be painted in the new blue colour and after naming worked the 1250 West of England express.

The BR Stock Building programme for 1949 was covered in some detail, amounting to 465 locomotives, 1972 coaches and 27,225 wagons. 309 of the locomotives were to be built in house with the remainder contracted out. New locomotives for the SR comprised –

2	Merchant Navy
15	Battle of Britain
5	Leader
1	Diesel mechanical shunter
15	350hp diesel electric
2	Mainline diesel electric

Finally, for June, mention was made of "The First Spotters' Excursion", which ran on 20th April from Waterloo to Portsmouth and return, the train being chartered by Ian Allan. The day was "*a glorious one and many parents – who presumably had obtained the necessary permission from their spotter sons - accompanied the party whose numbers included most of the members of the Ian Allan firm, from the Chief Spotter himself downwards.*"

JULY

On 25th May two of the new Travelling Tavern & Buffet sets, built to Bulleid's design, went on display at Waterloo. Eight of these new sets were to be operated on the ER and SR on the following services, Atlantic Coast Express, The Master Cutler, The White Rose, The Norfolkman – Cross Country Boat Train (Liverpool – Harwich) and The South Yorkshireman. Externally the cars were of striking appearance with leaded light windows set high in cream panelling, the lower half being in the new BR crimson lake coach livery lined out to represent brickwork. The cream panelling was broken by vertical black panels representing an old half-timbered inn, and set in the middle was an inn sign, the two on the SR being "White Horse" and "Jolly Tar". The other sets rejoiced in the names of "The Dolphin", "The Three Plovers", "The Bull", "The Salutation", "The Green Man" and "The Crown". Suspended from one of the roof beams in the Tavern Car was a small replica of this inn sign painted by Joan Main and David Cobb, who have specialised in the revival of this branch of art. In the 1st Class portion of the Restaurant car there was a radical departure from normal seating practice, in that seats faced inwards along the whole length of each side of the coach, with separate tables for each pair of seats. Another novel feature was the glass racks above the seats for light articles, the toughened glass having the great advantage that the passenger could easily see whether they had left anything behind ! A rider to the report mentioned that "*the reception given to the new Tavern cars has not been wholly favourable but bearing in mind the follow-my-leader habit of critics in most walks of life, also the number of times they prove to be out of touch with real public opinion, we prefer to adapt the old adage "The proof of the Tavern will be in its patronage*". (The Tavern Cars were not altered until 1959-60 when they were restyled as conventional kitchen-buffet cars with full size buffet windows).

Applications were invited from railwaymen's daughters between the ages of 14 and 16 for the title of "Railway Queen".

Travelling Tavern and Buffet
NOVEL RESTAURANT-BUFFET CARS BUILT AT EASTLEIGH.

Sampling in the "White Horse" (with snacks at the bar).

Eastleigh officials and staff responsible for the production trying-out the First Class Restaurant Car.

July, 1949.

Page 145

The daughter of any railwayman on British Railways is eligible as candidate to become Railway Queen.

CROWNING OF BRITAIN'S
R A I L W A Y   Q U E E N
Belle Vue Gardens, Manchester,
Saturday, September 24, 1949

The Railway Employees' Carnival is the Biggest One Day Event of its kind in the world. Continuous Attractions Midday to Midnight. Bands. Pipers. Orchestras. Concerts. Dancing. Sports. Carnival Parade. Football. Fireworks.

Candidates for Railway Queen must not be under 14 or over 16 years of age on September 1, 1949. Photographs must be received not later than August 27. Further details from the General Secretary, H. H. Neilson, 36, Sandown Lane, Wavertree, Liverpool, 15.

AUGUST

The "Maid of Orleans", the latest addition to the 130 strong BR fleet, entered the Folkestone – Boulogne Service on the 23rd June. Built by Denny of Dumbarton, Lady Missenden had launched the ship the previous September. It replaced a ship of the same name sunk by enemy action during the Normandy invasion.

An item headed "Cherries in Ice" told of the successful experiments carried out by the SR, when consignments of cherries for Glasgow and Cardiff were dispatched on Saturday afternoons from Rainham station in Kent loaded into insulated rail wagons containing dry ice. Despite very hot weather, the fruit was found to be "orchard fresh" when unloaded.

A stock of five million grain sacks was maintained by BR in the Eastern, LM, NE and Scottish Regions for hire to farmers who wish to forward grain. Previously a farmer hiring such sacks had to pay for them to be returned empty, but BR has now arranged that they may be handed in at any station, including those on the WR and SR where sack hiring is undertaken by private contractors.

The Southern Railway Company was the first of the former companies to cease to exist for, contrary to popular belief, the Big Four did not pass out of existence when the railways were nationalised on 1st January 1948. Before dissolution they had to prove that all their property had been transferred to the BTC, that all moneys in their hands had been properly distributed and that they had not entered into any agreement which the BTC may have cause to disclaim. The SR was the first to achieve these conditions and consequently this was "gazetted" by the Board of Trade on the 10th June 1949.

Small Ads were carried each month, a typical example, at 3d a word, being –

Blackpool – *Central. Bed, breakfast, high tea 10/6. Full Board 14/6. Running water all bedrooms. Lounge - Dining room. Separate tables. Near sea, amusements. Plenty of good food. Personal service. Mrs Chadwick, "Holmleigh" 28 Livingstone Road (Fireman's wife).*

SEPTEMBER

BR took the Booking Office to the beaches that summer with a road mobile office complete with tickets, timetables and travel literature, that toured the South Coast from Kent to Devon providing travel information and selling tickets for day, half day and evening excursion trips from local stations. The SR was the first region to experiment with this trailer van, which had living accommodation for staff, if required and was towed by a tractor unit. Beginning at Herne Bay, the Booking Office ended its journey at Exmouth travelling via the principal seaside resorts, including Brighton, Worthing, Bognor Regis, Bournemouth, Swanage, Weymouth, Lyme Regis and Seaton.

The Horsham – Guildford line was spotlighted in a lengthy article, continued the following month, each station and its staff being described in some detail. It is revealing to note that, even in 1949, traffic on this line was slight, the traffic returns for Slinfold, the first station after the junction at Christ's Hospital, for the first quarter of the year showed only 470 tickets were issued, giving an average of five or six passengers per day. There were just five season ticket holders. Most travellers had been lost to road transport, the hourly bus service to Horsham being more attractive than the eight a day railway service. The 2130 late service from

Horsham had been a casualty of wartime and the current last train at 7.12 pm was "brusquely *dismissed as performing neither of the functions of the former last train, ie to allow attendance at the cinema in Horsham or to enjoy a reasonably long day out at the seaside.*" Thus we see that criticism of the service provided was permitted by the magazine, which did not just give a favourable "spin" to items appearing in its pages. (The line did not close until 1965).

An item of an unusual nature had been handled at the SR's Deptford Wharf recently, when a massive 16 ton tree trunk was shipped to France via the SS Jupiter, using the wharf's 30 ton hydraulic crane.

OCTOBER

The annual International Timetable Conference, attended by delegates from over 20 countries, was held on Southern Region territory, at the Brighton Pavilion in October. The aim of the conference was to agree international services operating across Europe for the forthcoming year.

Big news of the month concerned the retirement of Oliver Bulleid, controversial CME of the Southern Region. Sir Eustace Missenden recalled the day 12 years before when Bulleid came to the Southern Railway and said they soon realised that they had a brilliant engineer, full of new ideas. He went on to say

that "*Mr Bulleid is the outstanding mechanical engineer in this country today and his name will be recorded with those of Churchward and Stanier and will always be associated with the Merchant Navy and Battle of Britain locomotives*" – (no mention of the Leader of course !). He was presented with "*a French silver-gilt dessert service in a brass bound case*" and, in replying to the many tributes, Bulleid recalled his career from the time he joined Doncaster Works in 1905. On that occasion his first contacts had been with workshop staff and it was perhaps fitting that the last thing he was going to do on the Southern Region was have dinner with the boilermakers !

Another naming ceremony took place at Waterloo on 20th September when 35025 Brocklebank Line was named by the Chairman of Messrs. Thos. & Jno Brocklebank Ltd, Colonel Dennis H Bates. The idea of naming this class of locomotive was to pay tribute to the masters, officers and crew of the merchant marine who lost their lives in the war. Brocklebank Line had apparently lost 60% of their fleet in the recent conflict but they had replaced all but two by the time of the naming ceremony.

A new factory for ice cream had recently opened in Sherborne and forwardings by rail, particularly to stations in South Devon, had been substantial. It is anticipated that output would be considerably increased by the next summer.

Above - Retirement presentation to OVS Bulleid. Centre is Mr John Elliot, with Bulleid to the right and Missenden to the left. Head and shoulders between Missenden and Elliot is S B Warder, the newly appointed Mechanical and Electrical Engineer for the Southern Region.

Right - Ice cream ready for loading at Sherborne.

Lower - The naming of 35025. A rather grubby driver (un-named) is seen shaking hands with Col Bates. Also present are T E Chrimes, S W Smart and R P Biddle.

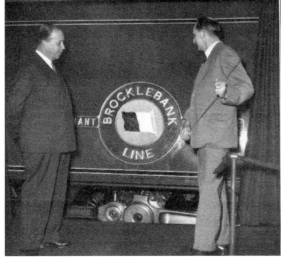

The third annual Public Day at the Longmoor Military railway was held on 3rd September, the 10th anniversary of the start of the last war. Newly named 34090 was a visitor at Ashford Works Open Day.

NOVEMBER

Under the Headline "A Great Leader of a Great Railway", this issue paid tribute to Sir Herbert Walker K C B, who had died on 29th September at the age of 81. He was General Manager at Waterloo from 1912 – 1937 personifying the ethos of the old "Southern". Flags flew at half mast on SR stations, docks and steamers and a memorial service was held at St Martins-in-the-Fields on 19th October. Sir Eustace Missenden, in his tribute in "The Times", said that he felt *sad and very lonely without that tall figure, with its measured step and friendly look coming again towards us."*

Locomotive News – New locomotives put into service –

West Country	34091 / 34092,
Diesel electric	15222

Locomotives withdrawn -

B1	1446 / 1448
D1	2253
K10	345
L11	167
O1	1374 / 1385 / 1429
G6	263

As part of its campaign to improve passenger travel the Railway Executive has arranged to provide, experimentally, liquid soap and paper towels in the toilet compartments of twelve main line expresses.

DECEMBER

Headlining this month's magazine was the first run of Bulleid's double-decker electric multiple units on 1st November, the inaugural train running from Charing Cross to Dartford and carrying notable guests, including Herbert Morrison (Lord President of the Council), Alfred Barnes (Minister of Transport), Sir Cyril Hurcomb (Chairman of the BTC), Sir Eustace Missenden (Chairman of the Railway Executive), John Elliot (CRO Southern Region) together with Bulleid himself (Retiring CME). The 8 car train, of twp 4 car units, numbered 4001 and 4002, was built at Lancing and Eastleigh and went into public service the following day providing 1104 seats compared with the 772 of a standard 8-car train set. The pair were scheduled to run in the following services on Mondays-Fridays and at suitable peak times on Saturdays –

07.05	Barnehurst – Charing Cross via Bexleyheath
07.50	Charing Cross – Crayford via Sidcup
08.30	Crayford – Cannon Street via Sidcup
09.16	Cannon Street – Dartford via Woolwich
10.09	Dartford – Charing Cross via Sidcup
10.58	Charing Cross – Dartford via Greenwich line
14.22	Slades Green – Cannon Street via Bexleyheath
15.17	Cannon Street – Gravesend Central via Woolwich
16.23	Gravesend Central – Charing Cross via Bexleyheath
17.35	Charing Cross – Barnehurst via Bexleyheath

With the benefit of hindsight, it is interesting to note the emphasis given in the article to determining whether the public took to the idea of the top deck, whether joining

A regular feature was "Our Gallery of Old Timers". This particular illustration was from the November issue and featured Guildford shed in 1907. The photograph was submitted by Motorman F W Sykes of Farnham, then an engine cleaner, who is standing by the steps ahead of the front splasher.

and alighting quickly from the coaches were achieved in service and, perhaps most importantly, in view of the future complaints in service regarding unpleasant odours (the noses of the lower deck passengers were in uncomfortably close proximity to the feet of the upper deck passengers), the importance attached to ventilation of the units. Loading gauge restrictions meant the windows on the upper deck could not be opened and the guard was charged with looking after the pressure ventilation system, having a rotary thermometer installed in his compartment, indicating how the heating and ventilation controls, installed in plenum chambers below the upper compartments, should be used.

A final mention for some of the regular advertisers who no doubt helped to keep down the costs of publication –

Osram Lamps
Double Diamond
Tudor Accumulators
Westons Biscuits
Henley Tyres
Pooley Weighing machines
Tudor Batteries

From January 1st 1950, each region was to have its own edition of a new British Railways Magazine, the major part of the 20 page monthly being devoted to news of a regional character. This new magazine was to be the direct successor to those magazines published by the former railway companies prior to January 1st 1948. Thus ended a short lived but fascinating episode in the history of staff magazines, which gave such an insight into the workings of the railways.

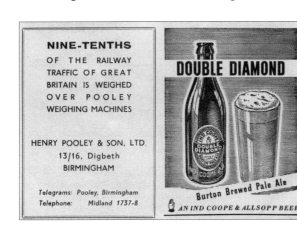
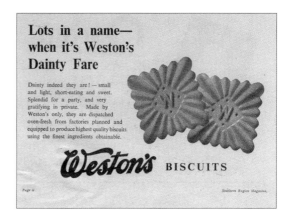

ALONG THE SUSSEX COAST - 80 YEARS AGO

John Cox

In 1923, at Grouping, the Southern Railway inherited a motley collection of rolling stock. At the time little electrification had taken place and many elderly locomotives from other companies were operating and having more general use over the ex LBSC lines.

The pictures in this article illustrate the wide variety of locos and stock that ran over the coast lines at this time. The actual illustrations, found in a job lot of black and white in an auction, give no clue as to who the photographer was, the places or dates when they were taken. However it has been possible to make certain assumptions and to identify a few of the locations. It seems the photos were taken in the late 1920s or possibly the early 1930s as several of the locomotives have not been renumbered in the 2xxx range, similarly some of the headcodes have given a clue as to destinations but not the actual trains. That said, an early shed allocation list has further given an idea of the various workings.

All of these views show what are more correctly referred to as SECR 'Trio' sets, the type seen, having the 'Birdcage' lookout, being the most common.

Opposite upper - *Taken from the beach at Galley Hill, Bexhill, an ex SECR Wainwright 'D' class passes Glyne Gap Gas Works with a westbound Ashford-Brighton working. This was a regular 'D' class duty. Behind the tender, and part of the train, is a 4-wheeled brake/luggage van. On a parallel line is a private owner wagon which, although it is not easy to make out, belongs to the St Leonards Gas Company.*

Opposite bottom - *Looking towards Bexhill at Glyne Gap, an eastbound train for Hastings is headed by a C2X No 440. Here the 'Birdcage' has been suppressed after Wainwright had resigned. These 'suppressed' sets were built in the period 1915-21 and additionally differed from previous sets in that there was no paneling and the brake vehicles had 8-compartments. Under the Southern these 1915-21 sets were renumbered 573, and 630-638.*

This page - *At an unidentified location, Gladstone class No 191,heads a neat three car 'Birdcage' set.*

A fine study of 'L1' No 782 speeding through Glynde with a 3-car set, west bound. Note the cattle trucks and tall signal beyond the bridge. The siding, bottom left, ran into the chalk pit. The centre vehicle appears to be an ex SECR 10-compartment third rather than the usual composite. What is interesting in nearly all the views is how, despite being so soon after grouping, LBSCR stock appears to have been swept away. Partly this was because of the LBSCR having fitted much of its stock with Westinghouse instead of vacuum brakes. Additionally and as found out by the SR to its cost later, the LBSCR coaching stock did not fare well if involved in an accident, even at comparatively slow speed, with fatal consequences for the unfortunate vehicle occupants.

Somewhere along the coastline, 'D3' tank No 363 hauls a motley collection of vehicles. The roof boards would indicate some form of through train shared with one of the other companies. Possibly, this is the Birkenhead working, which alternated between GWR and SR vehicles.. The leading vehicle is of the type illustrated on Page 27 of the 'Preview' issue of 'SW'.

Still in LBSC livery, an E4 tank hauls two 3-car sets westbound into Cooden Beach Station. Both are Trio sets, the rear one probably of the non 'Birdcage' type.

On what may have been an excursion or a through train to the midlands, an unidentified 'B4' hauls a rake of Midland clerestory stock.

Coming from Hastings, '13' No 28 slows for the station at Cooden Beach at the head of another 'Birdcage' set.

Ex LBSC 'B4' class No 51 heads a three coach set on a westbound Hastings Brighton working.

Still in LBSC livery, 'E4' No 478 pauses at Polegate on a westbound service. This time it is ex LBSCR stock that is seen, whilst the locomotive has clearly been vacuum fitted.

'D1' class No 283 on a Hastings motor train working of ex LBSCR vehicles..

Brighton class 'D3' No 481 heads a varied collection of stock on the Coast line. This will be seen to be the same rake of stock as was viewed earlier. The same comments thus apply whilst it is unfortunate it is not possible to read the destinations shown on the roof-boards.

An Eastbourne based 'E5' runs a coastline train consisting of trio set of 'Birdcage' stock and a Billington luggage van. This loco was dual fitted for through workings from other companies.

A very fine study of newly outshopped trio set No 519 hauled by Gladstone 0-4-2 No 193, with a Brighton luggage van in the rear.

With grateful thanks for additional caption information from Terry Cole and Gerry Bixley.

CERTAINLY NOT AN ESSAY IN CONCRETE, PERHAPS MORE OF A SENTENCE

Back in 1987, George Reeve and Chris Hawkins produced what was intended to be the first in the 'Southern Noveau' series of books. (Wild Swan 0906867479)

Having been unavailable for some years and we know somewhat sought after, it is appropriate to include a couple of pages of concrete items that are additional to the book. As ever, "...more WILL follow in the future", but any contributions you can make, which we might be able to include would also be most welcome.

In the lower view opposite, a first glance appears to show the workman painting the concrete, unlikely. His task is more likely to have been applying putty or sealant around the window.

(With grateful thanks to Andy Jupe).

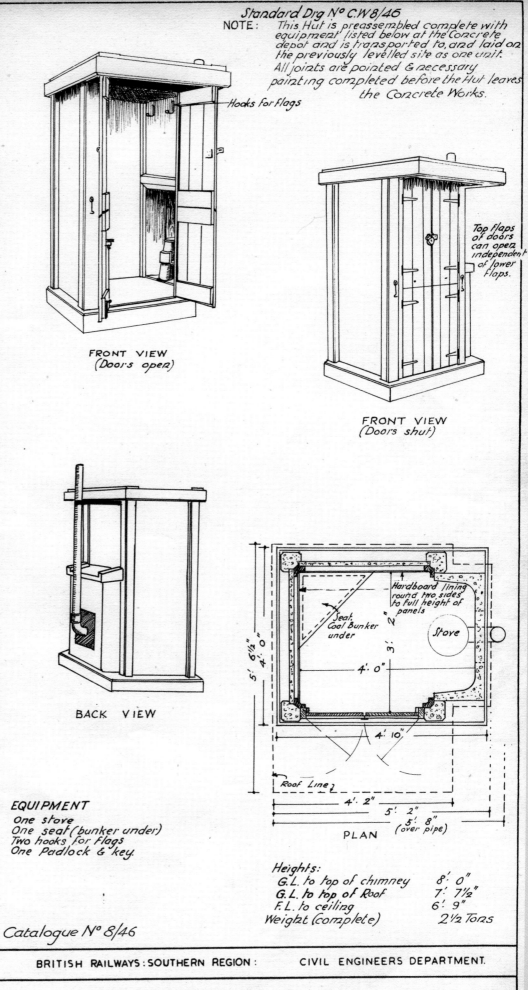

Standard Drg Nº C.W 8/46

NOTE: This Hut is preassembled complete with equipment listed below at the Concrete depot and is transported to, and laid on the previously levelled site as one unit. All joints are pointed & necessary painting completed before the Hut leaves the Concrete Works.

Hooks for flags

FRONT VIEW
(Doors open)

Top flaps of doors can open independent of lower flaps.

FRONT VIEW
(Doors shut)

BACK VIEW

Hardboard lining round two sides to full height of panels

Seat. Coal Bunker under

Stove

5' 6½"
4' 0"
3' 2"
4' 0"
4' 10"
4' 2"
5' 2"
5' 8" (over pipe)

Roof Line

PLAN

EQUIPMENT
One stove
One seat (bunker under)
Two hooks for flags
One Padlock & key.

Heights:
G.L. to top of chimney   8' 0"
G.L. to top of Roof   7' 7½"
F.L. to ceiling   6' 9"
Weight (complete)   2½ Tons

Catalogue Nº 8/46

BRITISH RAILWAYS : SOUTHERN REGION :   CIVIL ENGINEERS DEPARTMENT.

PRE-ASSEMBLED FOGMAN'S HUT

Once in a while something rather special turns up, such as here at Petersfield, sometime in 1884 / 1885. The view came courtesy of Barry Mursell and Crawley Model Railway Society, with a note that is was thought to be the Midhurst branch train. The obvious person to ask, of course, was Gordon Weddell, who confirms the train The vehicles are two 19ft x 7ft 7ins Firsts, then a 21 ft Second and another 19 ft First. The identity of the Passenger Brake Van is not absolutely certain, but it could well be a 22 ft van dating from the period 1871 to 1874. Whilst Gordon used a cut down version of this view taken from the 1904 *Railway Magazine* in his *LSWR Carriages Vol 1*, this is the first time that we are aware an original print, in its entirety, has come to light.

Further information has also come from Peter Swift, who advises the loco was rebuilt with a tender in 1885. The train would appear to be standing in the down siding with 'Petersfield Yard Signals' behind. This structure dates from around 1884, indeed the brickwork would appear new and dates from the period when large but narrow window panes were being used. The box was later reclassified as a Ground Frame, possibly around 1902, and probably lasted until the layout here was altered in 1929. The end of the station will also just be noted in the background.

Interestingly the original print, mounted on card, bears the name, 'T Wells, Portrait and Landscape Photographer (Late of Alton), West End Studio, near the Railway Station, Petersfield'.

With grateful thanks to all those mentioned for their assistance.

The propensity of the original Bulleid Pacifics to spontaneously combust is well known. What are perhaps less common are views of this actually happening, although one such occasion was caught on film here at Hamble Halt, on the line between Fareham and St Denys, on Whit Monday, 22nd May 1961. The engine was working the 9.40 am Brighton to Bournemouth West and came to grief close to Hamble Halt. The inferno was sufficient to warrant the attention of the fire brigade, crews from Hamble and Botley attending. The close proximity of the petroleum storage plant at Hamble no doubt meant they were in attendance quickly.

34057 has been liberally dosed with foam although, to be fair, the seat of the fire was hardly likely to have been on the exterior of the casing, and much more likely to have been underneath in the space filled with lagging around the boiler. The usual cause was oil from either a leaking oil bath or leaking pipes in this area soaking into the lagging and then being ignited by a spark from the brake blocks. The results could be dramatic and on occasions quite alien to a spectator. Witness the comment made by Peter Smith in his 'Mendips Engineman' book, when he refers to having to explain the reason for a delay of this type to a passenger. The mention that the engine had a fire in it was greeted with the retort, "Young man don't you know an engine always has a fire in it". On this occasion 34057 and its train were rescued by 76019 which arrived from the direction of Southampton at 12.00 and at 12.15 hauled the complete assembly to the next station, Netley, where 34057 was deposited in the yard and, according to the 'Railway Observer', left to 'simmer', still seemingly able to produce steam in quantity. Non-classified' repairs were effected at Eastleigh between the 6th and 17th June. Consequent delays were reported as having affected the booked return working from Bournemouth, as well as some Salisbury trains, which were diverted via Botley instead. Collection - The late Tony Sedgwick / Southampton Model Railway Club.

'Burning Bulleids'

a definite precursor to the article that follows……..

34064 with the 12.35 Waterloo to Bournemouth in Clapham Cutting, April 1966. Evidence of burning is apparent here too and it is unlikely much in the way of remedial painting would have been applied before the engine was withdrawn on 22nd May 1966. (According to the 'Book of the West Country and Battle of Britain Pacifics", the same locomotive spent the period from 16th March to 2nd May 1964 under Light Intermediate repair - puzzling.

Clive Groom

But to return to the title above and likewise the reason for the sub heading to this piece. What follows are the reminiscences of former Eastleigh Works and Shed fitter, Eric Best. He is forthright in his comments on certain machines, particularly the work of Mr Bulleid. But as the best periodicals say, "The views expressed by contributors do not necessarily represent the views of the Editor". So read on….

Above - 2325 the former 'Abergavenny' on the dump or scrap lines as they were called at Eastleigh running shed in 1945. This was the engine Eric had seen thundering down through Winchester a few years earlier. Despite its location it was reprieved and lasted in service until June 1951.

Below - No such reprieve for No 2040, seen at the same time and at the same location in September 1945. This was also the engine 'signed' by numerous enthusiasts. It was not cut up until some years later.

ERIC BEST

Memories of South Hampshire and a Railway Career...

As a youngster brought up in the delightful surroundings of the City of Winchester, I was fortunate to have the choice of watching trains at two stations. Very near to the family home was that of the Southern Railway, whilst across the City, on the eastern side, was the Great Western's example, Chesil.

One particularly memorable Saturday afternoon, during the early weeks of 1941, I was at the Southern station. This was the occasion of the very first trial run of the prototype Merchant Navy class pacific, No.21C1 *Channel Packet.* The strange looking, slab sided loco, approached the station running tender first. I remember thinking, "What the hell is this?" At that time it was painted grey with white stripes. Into the yard it slowly trundled. Then the unbelievable occurred, as all of it's vast reservoir of valve gear lubrication ran out from underneath. Presumably the gasket around the oil bath sump was not sealed tightly enough. (This was secured by fifty plus studded bolts, and still the loco was not oil tight!) I took an instant dislike to Bulleid's locomotives from that very first moment and I have never liked them since!

A short while after that event, 21C1 went up to Alresford on the Mid Hants line, where official photographs were taken. As a precaution against failure, it was the regular practice during the early life of *Channel Packet,* to accompany the new locomotive with a vintage Adams 4-4-0. This was an insurance policy, just in case it could not get back to Eastleigh, under it's own power. It was at Alresford, in the lowly cattle dock siding, that the photographic record was taken. There is a photograph extant with a fraction of an Adams loco visible in the background; although nine times out of ten, these pictures just show 21C1 on it's own. The first examples of the new Merchant Navys were to continue their association with the vintage Adams locomotives for a while longer. Two A12 Class 0-4-2's and one X6 Class 4-4-0 were converted to supply steam to pre heat the boilers of the new Pacifics. One of the A12's, No 612 still retained the pre war Maunsell livery, complete with gold lettering. Within a short period of time the practice of pre-heating was discontinued and the three unfortunate vintage locos made their final journey to the dump at Eastleigh running sheds.

To be fair, my preference was always for the Great Western's Chesil station. This was a very quiet affair when compared to it's neighbour up the hill. The build up to D-Day and the subsequent extending of the Normandy beach head resulted in a vast increase in the amount of traffic passing through the station. During the conflict, the former Didcot, Newbury and Southampton Railway line had been upgraded from a 'yellow' restricted route to 'blue'. Throughout the first half of 1944 there was an incessant flow of heavy goods traffic passing through the station, heading for various disposal dumps located near to the South Coast. Following the successful invasion, most of this traffic would be bound for the docks at Southampton. Numerous classes of locomotives were to be seen throughout this hectic period. Most common were the 53xx moguls, ROD 2-8-0's and Hall class 4-6-0's. To my young eyes, the rarest examples were No. 7813 *Freshford Manor* and an outside framed Aberdare Class 2-6-0. Both of these were the only sightings I made of these classes on this route. The Manor appeared from out of the gloom of the tunnel that graced the northern end of the station. Through the station it trundled with a goods train, then for some inexplicable reason it ran slowly into the goods yard, after a short pause left it, and continued on it's journey southwards. No sooner had it departed, then another heavily laden freight train appeared, because the invasion was in full swing at that time. The Halls and Aberdares were designated as red route restricted engines, which begs the question as to how they slipped through the net.

Occasional forays were made via the DNS line

We are delighted to present the reminiscences of former Eastleigh Fitter Eric Best. Eric is known for his forthright comments on certain types of Southern (and other) locomotives, based not on personal preference, but on the practicalities of maintaining them. You might find your own personal favourite is not perhaps his first choice....!
Eric is also renowned for his skills as a model engineer having built several 5" gauge models. He is also the proud owner of a restored traction engine.

to the GWR West of England main line at Newbury station. The early morning northward bound journey was invariably made behind a Collett 22xx class 0-6-0. I remember a large poster, prominently displayed at the doorway to 'Chesil station, proclaiming, "Is your journey really necessary?" The answer was "yes", I wanted to see some big Great Western locos! The first time I went to Newbury, the station pilot was Castle Class 4-6-0 No. 4037 *The South Wales Borderers*. At that time it was allocated to Reading shed, and had gained a reputation as a poor performer.

On occasions, when I had a little more money in my pocket, I would extend the jaunt to Reading. I could have gone to Reading by the Southern, which was by far the shorter route, but much preferred going via the 'Western'. This latter way took about two and a half hours - barmy! Going this way, within a short distance after leaving Newbury, the racecourse was passed, a large area of which had been covered with temporary sidings. Here were stabled a substantial number of locomotives, amongst these numerous WD 2-8-0's and 0-6-0 tanks. The latter carried the inscription of the United States Transportation Corps on their sides.

One particular post war Saturday morning, was typical. I was standing on one of the two platforms at Chesil. A regular working at that time was for an M7 Class 0-4-4 tank. This came up from Eastleigh, light engine, and would then run into the horse dock. Here it would await the arrival of the down mid-day passenger train from Didcot. As was the practice at that time, the GW loco would come off of the train and run the short distance down to the small loco shed. In those far off days the GW did not always run right through to Southampton, hence the use of the Southern Drummond tank to take the train forward. The GW loco, having completed it's week's work, would stay on the shed until the following Monday morning.

Whilst waiting for the mid day arrival, the vintage tank engine would, if required, perform a spot of shunting or other tasks. I was talking to the driver on this particular occasion when one of the station staff approached. The driver was informed that he was wanted in the yard, where he was to pick up some wagons which required running up to the gas works, which was just beyond the northern portal of the tunnel. The friendly driver turned to me and asked, "Do you want a ride?" "Too right", came my speedy reply and with that I climbed aboard. "Park yourself somewhere over there," commented my new friend and pointed to the opposite rear corner of the cab. Whilst the loco moved down to the yard, the fireman busied himself with his duties. A dozen or so loaded coal wagons were picked up and, in no time at all, we were trundling back through the station and entering the sulphurous gloom of the tunnel. The loaded coal wagons were dropped off at Winnal Gas Works, a

spot of shunting was performed, and finally a few empties were coupled on to the rear. Then, all too soon as far as I was concerned, the Drummond tank retraced it's way through the tunnel and the empty wagons were dropped of in the yard.

Within minutes my very first footplate trip was to come to an end as the station was approached. For a second time that morning, the M7 came to a stand in the horse dock siding. Fortunately for the crew, there was sufficient time to spare for a well earned bite to eat, before the journey down to Southampton commenced. The driver then asked me if would like a cheese sandwich. Until that very moment in time I had hated cheese, but there was no way that I was going to offend this kind gentleman, and so enthusiastically, "Yes please." Funnily enough I thoroughly enjoyed it!

Visits to Eastleigh shed as a lad were fairly routine during those early post war years, as was the inevitable bunking. When we were kids, there used to be a pointsman who controlled the movements of the engines coming out of the coaling stage These invariably required turning on the triangle, before running back towards the shed. This man had a little hut there and we used to get across the track at this point, so that we could get amongst the two 'dump' lines of dead engines that were situated over at the far side. All of this had to be accomplished without being spotted. We would wait, hidden in the long lineside grass, until the pointsman wandered away. Then within an instant, we to would be gone, right across the tracks to the distant row of withdrawn locos.

One long term resident amongst the two lines of decrepit wrecks was the former 'Brighton' Atlantic No. 2040. This engine had been laid aside back in 1939 but did not get cut up until ten years later. It was unique amongst the two classes in that it had the cylinder drain cock pipes running along the outside, supported by brackets. The remainder had their pipes diverted to run between the bogie and the frames, where they met underneath, in the centre of the loco. With the post war increase in the value of scrap metal, it was rather strange that the scrap lines had to await the start of the fifth decade before being sorted out. This Atlantic, which had once been amongst the elite of the LBSCR main line stock, was suffering a great indignity at this time. There was a craze amongst the local train spotting fraternity, which lasted for a few years, of writing our names in pencil all over the sides of the engine. Countless individuals had done so, consequently the faded paintwork was literally covered in graphite.

During the first couple of years after the cessation of hostilities, Nos 2325 and 2326 were also to be found on the back road of the dump. These fine 'Brighton' tanks had once carried the names of *Abergavenny* and *Bessborough* respectively. Having

The A12 seen working at Winchester with different numbers on the locomotive and tender, 625 and 637.

become redundant on their former native lines, they were to end their lives working from Basingstoke shed. I recall just a solitary sighting of one at work. This was No.2325, as it came thundering down through Winchester station at the head of a wartime van train. The livery was dark olive green, with black and white lining, all of which had faded with time. The dump lines were not confined to withdrawn locomotives, they also contained examples waiting to go into the works. Fortunately, Nos 2325 and 2326 were destined to 'go inside' and to be returned to traffic.

Another notable sighting at the SR's Winchester station, again towards the end of hostilities, was that of an Adams A12 'Jubilee'. I was standing on the cattle dock, as the loco ambled into the station from the north. It was working a lightly loaded pick up goods that had originated from Alton. The loco took the points that led into the goods yard, where it was required to perform a spot of shunting. Surprisingly, the engine and tender carried two different numbers. The loco was No. 637, whilst the tender proclaimed No. 625. Unfortunately, within a year, on the 3rd March 1946, this vintage machine was withdrawn from traffic. It was cut up during February 1948.

The end of hostilities saw the resumption of banana imports at Southampton Docks, complete with their very fast train workings. The fruit was still green when unloaded from the ships. To keep the ever ripening stems in good condition, steam heated, four wheeled covered vans were used. It was late one dark evening, that I saw the first such working with a T14, (a rebuilt Drummond 'Paddlebox' 4-6-0), on the front. It was pitch black at the time but up through the deep cutting came the magnificent sound of a large steam engine, obviously being worked very hard. The sound of the exhaust could be heard long before I set eyes upon the loco. Roaring up through the cutting, as it approached the station, it produced a firework display, the like of which I have never seen before or since.

Another memorable 'cop' was that of a 'Brighton' I3 tank, No. 2083. I arrived home that afternoon extremely pleased with myself, totally ignoring the fact that as a result of the very heavy rain that morning, I was soaked to the skin. Full of joy, I started to tell my father how I had been so very lucky to have seen this rare tank engine, only to be told in no uncertain terms, "What an idiot, look at the state of you"!

Nearer to home was another fine vantage point for watching passing traffic. This was the top of a bank that overlooked Winchester's GW running shed at Bar End. Here, in about 1946, the last working example of an ex LSWR X6 4-4-0, No. 658 came trundling round St Catherine's Hill, whilst working the Didcot bound pick up goods. Fitted with a Drummond boiler, it was painted in dark olive green, with Bulleid lettering. 'Locomotives Illustrated' stated that this engine ran it's final years in black livery, but this was definitely not so.

Steam was certainly in my blood, as apart from watching trains, traction engines and road rollers were another occupation at that time. My second cousin owned four traction engines, two 'Burrells', one 'Allchin', and one 'Marshall'. Thankfully one of the Burrell's still survives, although now in Yorkshire. An added bonus was that my friend's father looked after the fine beam engines at the City's sewage works. Many happy hours were spent there, watching two engines built by Gimpsons of Leicester - superb pieces of machinery.

I left school in 1948 at the age of fifteen and never went through the normal channels of finding employment. Of my own volition, I went down to the Works at Eastleigh and asked for a job. Fortunately all went well and my wish was granted -well almost! My first choice was to have become a sign writer. Instead of that, I was offered a non-indentured engineering / fitting

No 0334, 'Daphne' and the boilerless remains of 0332 on the scrap line. No 0332 had arrived at Eastleigh as far back as 20ᵗʰ May 1932. The bunker side of the 'A1' will be noted to have corroded right through. Later on the same engine, the chimney literally snapped off, again due to corrosion. To the right is the entrance to a wartime air-raid shelter.

apprenticeship, of five years duration. This would commence on my sixteenth birthday. In the meantime I could spend the rest of that year working in the print room.

Thus in January I started work as an office boy. The print room came under the jurisdiction of the drawing office, all of which was under the charge of Mr Mills. His successor in later years was Mr Stone, whilst the Works Manager at that time was Mr Munns. The prints were dyeline - blue prints. These were produced with amongst other substances, copious amounts of strong smelling ammonia.

What annoyed me, and still does now, was that I could have printed copies of anything that I had wanted. There were drawers ceiling high. You would pull these out and inside were masses of linen drawings, Adams 4-4-0's, and proposed locomotives that were never to see the light of day. Strangely enough, Mr Urie's Caledonian drawings were also in there. There were proposals for a 2-6-0 by Urie. This would have been a lovely little engine, very handsome indeed. He also designed a 4-4-2 express tank engine using a D15 boiler, with 6ft 7½ inch driving wheels, utilising his standard motion as on the larger G16 and H16 tanks.

During the slack periods, when there was very little work to do, I would be in there going through the drawers - fantastic! As well as the main room that housed the printing machinery, in an annex, was an adjoining room that was kept permanently locked. Despite the very best attempts at security, I found a way in there. It transpired that, between this secure room and the next one, were two adjoining cupboards. A pair of outward opening doors, just large enough for my torso, so gained me access. Through the back of the cupboard and then up through the roof, I would go, by which means I could get into the forbidden room.

In this room were Locomotive and Railway Magazines going right back to their respective first issues. These were in large dusty piles. Many happy hours were spent there. The funny thing was that I could hear my colleagues in the adjoining room saying, "… Where's that nipper gone, where's he disappeared too? I never did let them know my secret.

During the early nineteen sixties, when all steam engine construction had ceased, these rooms were cleared out. A covered van was placed below one of the windows, into which much of this veritable Aladdin's Cave was emptied. As fast as the contents from that

All that remained of Drummond's 'Bug' in 1945, the chassis and bogies. In this fashion it ended its days as a means of moving lengthy items around the works.

hidden room went into one side of the van, so many of us would be removing them through the opposite doors!

The dark room was located in the opposite side of the building from the printing room. In there the entire, priceless collection of negatives was stored. All on glass, these went back in time to when Eastleigh Works had started in 1909. Here was, amongst other subjects, the complete photographic record of every single locomotive that had been constructed there. Needless to say, this was another source of rummaging by this fifteen year old lad.

During the late nineteen thirties Eastleigh had embarked on the first steps leading towards the creation of a museum. The 'Bug' and 0-6-0 saddle tank No.0334 were the first residents. Also kept there was the highly burnished T9 4-4-0 Royal Train locomotive, No. 119. Unfortunately, all of this was to come to nothing, and the former pair was to be found languishing at the back of the works at the time I commenced working there. No 0334 stood there until about 1949/50. Also languishing in the scrap lines was the former 'Brighton' A1 Class 0-6-0 tank *Daphne*, which had come from the Shropshire and Montgomeryshire Railway.

Despite all of the early wartime appeals for metal, when householders had willingly donated their pots and pans and their wrought iron railings, Eastleigh's long lines of withdrawn engines were not cut up. No 10

Daphne had been withdrawn as long ago as 1936 and was not to be dismantled until 1949. An even older relic, the same age as No 0334, was 0-6-0 saddle tank No. 0332. This example had been fitted with a Drummond boiler but this item was later removed, being placed instead on East Kent Railway No 4. The frames and wheels of No 0332 had stood there since being withdrawn from traffic as long ago as 1933!

Lunchtimes would find my office colleagues and me on our way outside to play on these derelict engines. On one particular occasion it was the diminutive 'Daphne' that was to receive our undivided attentions. My friend made the mistake of hiding in the locomotive's smokebox, thinking that I was unaware of this. Unfortunately for him I was only too aware of where he was and firmly closed the smokebox door. The next thing was to find a supply of water nearby, which I commenced to pour down the chimney. It was a very wet and dirty friend that returned to work. Unfortunately, embarrassing questions were asked as to how this had occurred.

An unusual sight in the works yard at that time, were four former LNWR tenders. Two were of the vintage 'Whale' variety, whilst the others had come off a pair of Bowen Cooke's 'Claughton' class 4-6-0's. These latter examples carried the full LMS livery. Both had been converted for oil storage; the large tanks standing proud of the tender tops. My impression is that these were used on the Southern prior to customised oil storage facilities being installed. Another tender that languished within the Works, was from another 'Brighton' Atlantic No. 2041. The actual loco was cut up in 1947, but for some unexplained reason the tender lasted until 1949. This was eventually taken from Eastleigh, along with a lot of other stock, to Dinton, where all met their inevitable fete.

Within the Works, in No 4 bay, were examples of the former USA tank engines that I had witnessed dumped at Newbury Racecourse, just after the war. These were being converted for use as shunters in the Docks at Southampton. Fifteen examples were purchased, although only fourteen entered traffic. No. 1264 was used as a source of spares. Examples of the elderly B4 tanks were still being used there at this time, although, for the majority, their days were numbered.

O. V. S. Bulleid's first 'Leader' Class loco No. 36001 appeared at the Works during 1949. Up to that point it had been performing trial running from Brighton. A multitude of teething troubles had occurred, so it was given one last chance, at Eastleigh. Having appeared over the course of a weekend, the following Monday morning found most of the staff gazing out of the windows at this very strange machine. I was one of the perplexed spectators. It was a big, ugly, grey thing, - "What the hell is that?" we all exclaimed in utter astonishment! I knew nothing of it's existence. "That's to replace an M7 tank", came an assured reply from one of the more knowing men in the crowd!

"What are you talking about?", was my reply, in utter disbelief. 36001 was forever in and out of the Works. My mate saw it running up through Winchester with a trailing load of approximately six coaches. We eventually heard that it did not return until the following day. It transpired that it had run out of water. It was put into Micheldever where it was filled with a half inch hose!

On one memorable occasion, I passed O.V.S. Bulleid on the stairs. I didn't know who he was. He was just an important man who wore glasses. I politely said good morning and continued up the stairs. When you are a 'nipper' these 'big wigs' intimidate you, so you keep a

Two of the four former LNWR tenders that arrived at Eastleigh, circa 1947, in connection with the abortive oil-firing episode of the time. The tenders arrived without tanks. These were fitted at Eastleigh. Exactly why the Southern should go to the bother of purchasing them at this time is a mystery, especially as it would have been thought they could have located sufficient of their own, the tenders from the withdrawn Brighton Atlantics for example? These were only used for a short time until superseded by the permanent, albeit short lived, storage facility.

The last of Mr Bulleid's 'Merchant Navy' class was being erected at Eastleigh during Eric's time as an apprentice. This is No 35030, later named 'Elder-Dempster Lines' and which entered service in April 1949.

low profile. He didn't put in much of an appearance at Eastleigh. I only saw him the once.

My first year came to an end and I was put into the fitting shop. There I was to stay for approximately two years, spending six months at a time with the various gangs. This was the point at which my apprenticeship started. Photographs taken inside this building during the first year of the Works existence show that very little had changed over the intervening years, the bench that I started working on being clearly depicted.

I was not a premium apprentice, which meant that no indentures were signed. The first gang that I went into was that of Bert Smith. Bert's was one of a pair of gangs employed on brakes. As a fitter / erector, no machinery was used, so I never went into the machine shop for any training.

All the work was very filthy. Dismantling a locomotive's brake gear involved removing the pins, knocking out the steel bushes and cleaning out all of the oil holes. All of the stripped out components, such as motion, brake gear and valve gear, would go into the 'bosh'. This was a large square tank that was filled with a very strong mixture of caustic soda. The purpose of this was to break down the layers of compacted dirt, rust and grease, etc. All of these components would go in there before coming onto the benches. The men that worked

the 'bosh' were a separate gang, we just took the components to them. The large cleaning tank was heated by a stationary boiler, which had been constructed at the Works. The boiler was situated outside of the building, being fed by an injector and a weir pump.

Problems arose with the condenser / heat exchanger, which used to become furred up. Remedial work on this piece of equipment was carried out at weekends or during bank holidays. This would involve removing the cover, cleaning the tubes and then reassembling. If for any reason the boiler had to be shut down, either an O2 0-4-4T or a G6 0-6-0T would be drafted in, necessitating plumbing the loco into the bosh. Returning to the brake gear, it was another person's task to reassemble the refurbished sets, which would require the pressing in of new bushes.

The coupling and connecting rod gang came under the leadership of George Fen. Cliff Pinns was in charge of firehole doors. Encompassed in this role were Bulleid's steam operated sliding doors. James's gang dealt with valve gear. George Robey repaired and refurbished the regulator heads, whilst finally there was Fred Cowley. His was the role of overhauling mechanical lubricators, Westinghouse brakes and safety valves. These first two years certainly produced a great variety of work. It was only George Robey's gang that I never worked in.

All of an apprentice's training and further education came under the jurisdiction of Reg Curl. Maths was studied during evening classes, which occurred at a nearby school. From day one, I had protested that all of the algebra that I was being forced to master, was an absolute waste of time. Unfortunately for me my protestations were to no avail, at least during those early years. Day release at Southampton Technical College came next, which meant I had the opportunity for long periods of absence from classes, watching trains and the steam powered floating bridges. Inevitably, this came to the attention of Reg Curl and resulted in a long and forthright discussion. The outcome was that it was agreed, by both of us, that there would be no more classroom work.

It was at this period in time, that I experienced my first true footplate ride on the DNS line. There were two sets of footplate crews at Winchester Chesil. One of the drivers was Tommy Keenan, who lived near to the shed. Tommy had had the great misfortune to have been shot and seriously wounded at the Dardanelles, during the ill fated Gallipoli Campaign, of the Great War. He had spent the whole of a frightening night, crawling round in a circle, in 'No Man's Land', only to find himself back where he had started. Fortunately rescue came and he recovered from his bullet wound.

Tommy was the driver of the vintage GWR outside framed 4-4-0 No. 9083 *Comet,* on that special day and the working was the Saturday 8.14 am departure from Winchester Chesil to Newbury. The crew on this duty from Winchester exchanged footplates with a pair of men that were working a Southampton bound goods train. This changeover occurred at a point mid-way up the line. Tommy Keenan also had a claim to fame on the celluloid screen. For it was he who drove the loco in the first making of the film 'The Ghost Train'.

Returning to Eastleigh, the scrap line has already been mentioned. Indeed a scrap line at Eastleigh had existed for decades. After the Great War, lines of withdrawn locos had stood there for many years. H.C. Casserley could not believe that all of these old classes still existed, even in the dumps. In total he must have taken over two hundred photographs of these decaying engines. There was one such line of these locos, running between the Works, which was completely full for years. One example had been withdrawn in 1914 and still languished there until 1925, retaining a very faded Drummond livery. Going further back in time, there remained numerous examples of both Adams's and Beattie's products, that had escaped the earlier Great War's drive for scrap metal.

At that time the newly formed Southern Railway was starting to withdraw Drummond 4-6-0's. Alongside these could be seen long withdrawn members of the '0145' Class 4-4-0 tanks. Surprisingly, all of them still retained their works plates, even when their boilers had been removed. The latter was exemplified by an example with a large curved Beyer Peacock brass plate surmounting the centre wheel splasher.

Returning to 1951 and the scrapping of locomotives, normally all such dismantling and cutting had been dealt with outside, at the rear of the Works. In 1951, when I was an apprentice, they cut up my pet engine, which was the 'Brighton' 4-6-2T *Bessborough*. This met it's fate in No 4 bay, within the Works. They had a night shift on then, and were concentrating on scrapping the former oil burners, K10's, L11's and T9's etc. Three and sometimes four locos would be reduced to piles of scrap each night. To cope with this vast influx of work, quite a large gang was put on the night shift. The whole place used to reek when you turned up for work in the morning, as it backed onto the fitting shop. When the cutters started to work below the cab floors, all the congealed oil and dirt would produce a very thick black smoke, in the manner of burning rubber. Having spent all night cutting up these loco's, there would be huge piles of rubble which, invariably, would consume all of the following day to clear away. Once removed, another batch of engines would be brought in. Amongst these unfortunate examples were HI Class 4-4-2's.

Working conditions 'inside' were fairly good. There used to be 'fat scrapers' employed. These were men whose sole task was to continually clean all of the oil and grease from the wooden floors. Constantly these individuals were to be seen, chipping away at the filthy deposits, using a tool not too dissimilar to a garden hoe. Theirs was a never ending task.

Working in the superheater gang was a shocking task. Firstly the elements had to be pulled from the boilers. Then came a bout of very thorough internal cleaning. You can imagine all the muck that there was in a superheater. They would be all scaled up, with an ample covering of soot on the outside to boot. All the muck in the world seemed to come out of these elements. After cleaning and repairing, came the testing. Firstly they were hydraulically pressurised. Then the fun started to begin, as you clouted them on the end, to ensure that they were sound. Any weakness was soon apparent, as copious amounts of water would be everywhere.

Six months were spent in this department, working under a very nasty chargehand, Will Thorne. A severe illness resulted in Will having to leave his job, which, in turn, found his son taking over as the head of the gang. Dick Thorne was so different from his father, a real gentleman. I was to be reunited with Dick Thorne many years later when be both found ourselves working at the Ford motor plant at nearby Swaythling.

A further transfer found me working in Bert Croot's boiler mounting gang. Here the pads were made

Another long term resident of the Eastleigh scarp line, X6 No 657 which had been withdrawn from general service as early as September 1940. This particular engine had featured in the wonderful 'Oh Mr Porter' film. It was later given a partial reprieve having been stripped of certain parts, was used to supply steam to the new Merchant Navy class engines at Exmouth Junction shed. It only performed this role for a few months and was laid aside at the Devon shed until March 1944, when it was towed to Eastleigh and dumped as seen above. Here it rusted away until finally broken up at Horley, in November 1949.

in the machine shop and riveted to the boiler. Our job was to face them to take the fittings. They produced all the pads for the boiler mountings on the LMS boilers that were in process of being constructed in the Works. The actual loco's, numbered in the 42xxx series, were constructed at Brighton.

Also produced within the works, for these new engines, were the con rods and valve gear. Each apprentice fitter had the job of making all the radii on these rods. When machined these had very sharp edges. Eastleigh men did not have grinders in those days. Instead we had to chip the rods with a hammer and a chisel, for a quarter of an inch, along the complete side and edge. Following this was the task of drawing and filing along the length of the rod, to get the correct radius. To get the correct curve, a little $\frac{1}{8}$th gauge was used. We were expected to make all of them to the same degree of curvature along their entire length and for this we were allowed half an hour. The fluting of the rods though was a machine procedure. Later when I went into the horn cheeks gang it was the same, hand chipping and filing. Another hand job was cutting the grooves in axle boxes, this time using a round nosed chisel. With such hard, labour intensive work, it was no surprise when

many lads did not return to Eastleigh Works after completing their National Service.

I was at Eastleigh at the time of the incident involving Merchant Navy Class Pacific No. 35020, hauling the 4.30 pm passenger working from Exeter Central, to Waterloo, on 24th April 1953. The train was gaining momentum as it came down the hill towards Crewkerne, when suddenly it's driving axle fractured. Fortunately the loco stayed on the rails and no injuries to the passengers occurred. As a result of this, all the Bulleid Pacifies were withdrawn, until a full examination of each engine could be carried out. To cover this serious loss of motive power, numerous locos were borrowed from the Midland and Eastern regions. This resulted in the unusual sight of Stanier Back Fives and Gresley V2's working express trains on the Southern Region. The latter were to be seen on such trains as the 'Bournemouth Belle', where they turned in some very fine performances.

I was working in the axle box gang at the time with Alver Casper in charge, although to everyone he was known as Albert. Following the temporary withdrawal of the Pacifies, we had crank axles coming into the works from everywhere, some were even arriving on lorries! They were just removing them at the running sheds and wheeling them in to us. Of course we had to re-fit all of the axle boxes again. I am remember that the Merchant Navy's were not the only examples of Bulleid's locomotives that had suffered from this serious problem. The infamous Leader did the same thing during it's short tenure at Eastleigh and confirmed my opinion that Bulleid engines were horrible, terrible things. It was also at about this time that the ultra sonic testing of axles was introduced at Eastleigh works. This was performed under the watchful eyes of Archie Croft.

As well as being in charge of the aforementioned gang, Alver Casper was also the AEU convener at that time. Somehow he managed to get a hold over everybody, whilst also arranging for no end of overtime for everyone who worked for him. Some times all of us, apprentices and all would be slaving away until ten at night.

We also had what were known as 'Finishing off gangs'. For example, a King Arthur would come into the Works with a hot box. We would have the problem wheels out and then taken over to the machine shop. When they were returned we would put them back under the engine. Following this, the loco would be taken out on the road for a test run, as far as Fareham.

As part of the learning process I continued to move between the gangs and eventually found myself in Bill Forest's frame gang. There was one very memorable occasion, I recall, a very warm summer's evening, when I was working overtime. We were involved in putting the valve liners into a Remembrance Class 4-6-0. These locos were conversions from the very elegant former LBSCR express tank engines.

In those days, we had a cast liner which was a neat fit to the valve cylinder bore. The method of insertion was as follows. A very substantial bolt was placed through the liner, with a sturdy plate attached at the rear end. Numerous plates were then attached to the front. A very large ratchet spanner was then used, to pull the liner in with brute force. There were approximately eight men, all struggling to pull the liner through and all perspiring heavily, due to the very tough task. Similar work today would see the liner frozen and shrunk before insertion. There was plenty of overtime in this department, which always came in handy although, unlike in some of the other departments, it was voluntary whether an individual worked these extra hours.

The final part of my five years was spent in Sid White's gang. This was the unhappiest place to work. Sid was a veritable giant of a man. Of stocky build, he must have been at least six foot six inches tall. It was quite comical to see him riding his tiny moped up the road to work. Even the poor unfortunate underpowered machine looked totally oppressed!

Sid was an ogre to all, including his family, so the story went. But none more so than to me. No matter what I, or any other unfortunate apprentice did, everything was wrong. Constantly, almost weekly it seemed, I would be summoned to the foreman's office for a reported offence. It the truth was told, the foreman, Mr Beesley, probably sympathised with his junior. For such a veritable tyrant, it was rather ironic, that Sid's passion was for growing Chrysanthemums. This was so out of keeping with his character.

Such, then, was a memorable apprenticeship, which I completed in 1955. Unfortunately I was only to earn the full rate of pay for a mere six weeks, as National Service beckoned. Like so many other railwaymen at that time, I applied for the Royal Engineers at Longmoor, but the army knew best and I was drafted into the Royal Artillery.

I returned to Eastleigh Works in 1957, but it would not be a happy homecoming. That very first shift commenced with me standing before the desk of Mr Beesley, the erecting shop foreman. "You know where you are going, don't you?" exclaimed the foreman. "Don't tell me," was my short reply although already my stomach had started to drop. Without being told another word, I guessed it was back to that unhappiest of places, Sid White's gang. Unfortunately nothing had changed and I would be in the office once a week. I was his whipping boy.

Most of the fitters would have preferred to have been employed on the 'new work' gang. At that time they were rebuilding the Bulleid Pacifies, although to get into the gang, you had to know somebody who was working there. That was also where the big money was being earned.

During the summer of 1957 there was a shortage of work for Sid's gang. No doubt as a result of this, I was taken to one side by Sid and told, "You are going out into the yard," meaning the scrap yard. "Fair enough," I replied, "Is anybody else coming?" I probably knew the answer already, "No, you are on your own," came the curt reply.

The scrap yard gang at Eastleigh Works had one member at the time, Dick Mitchell, a boilermaker by trade, had been employed there for a number of years, as it had always been the Works policy to use one of the latter tradesmen for operating the gas cutting equipment. The actual boiler smith's gang was headed by Joe Early. Under his direction, these artisans went around to the various departments, where they would perform a multitude of cutting and welding tasks. There was also a specialist welders shop, situated adjacent to the tool room. At that period this was a new set up department. The staff employed here were dedicated to this one place of work, except for going out to perform welding work on the frames of locos etc.

An '0395' or what was left of it and complete with asbestos lagging. The table on the next page records Eric having worked on dismantling two members of the class in 1958 and which means this could well be the remains of either 30564 or 30568.

As would be expected, staff accommodation in the scrap yard was primitive, consisting of an elderly wooden hut. Even so, in the depths of winter we would shelter inside for a body warming cup of tea. If Sid's intention had been to create a hostile working environment for me outside, then he failed, as from the very first day I enjoyed this new outdoor task, more so because I was away from my old adversary. The first days spent there saw the two of us reduce a couple of Urie King Arthur's to scrap. Unfortunately for me, whilst all of this had been going on the workload had built up inside, so it was back inside to Sid's gang again.

The following year I heard a whisper from the labourer in Les Norris's domain that plans were afoot to build up a scrapping gang, consisting of mates and fitters. Better still was the news that all of the staff to be employed out there were to come under the jurisdiction of Les. An added bonus was that regular overtime would be available, working inside during the evenings.

Within a short period of time, I was in Mr Beesley's office. "What's this I have been hearing, about

there being plans to build up a scrapping gang, down the bottom?" I asked. "That's right, are you interested?" "Too right", I replied. "Well, the money's no good." retorted the Foreman. "It's got to be a sight better than working with him.....", I continued. We concluded our conversation with Mr Beesley's final words, "Alright, fair enough, I'll get you transferred to Les Norris's gang."

Les was the charge hand over what basically consisted of the unfit, the lame and the lazy. The extra hours at premium rates, spent inside on overtime, more than compensated for the drop in wages that resulted from my escape from the clutches of Sid White. Les's gang was situated at the top of number four bay. It was ironic that an enlarged scrapping gang would not in the end occur for a few years, in the sixties, when steam was being decimated.

Rebuilt and repaired locomotives that had been dispatched back into traffic, were still under the jurisdiction of the Works as far as repairs were concerned for a number of weeks. These repairs, which were usually

Last days for 32424, which, from Eric's list below, was despatched on 26th May 1958.

carried out over in the running shed, were one of the varied roles that were performed by Les's gang. One memorable task was on an H15 4-6-0. A leak had developed on the boiler feed water pipe. This component consisted of three pieces, connected together by two joints. What should have been a very straight forward job, would in the end take the whole of one Saturday's overtime shift to rectify.

I was destined to spend six years working in the scrap yard during which time Dick and I had the task of scrapping the former Brighton Atlantic, 'Beachy Head'. Always a passionate lover of locomotives that emanated from the LBSCR, this example had been a favourite of mine. My actual role in it's demise was to remove all of a locomotive's fittings, whilst Dick 'drove the gas axe'. As far as I was concerned, to cut up this fine 4-4-2 was an act of sacrilege. *Beachy Head* had worked it's last duty, heading an enthusiasts special to Eastleigh, after which, the coaching stock was taken to Micheldever sidings, whilst the doomed Atlantic ran back onto the running sheds, where the fire was dropped for the very last time.

Eventually *Beachy Head's* turn came to be dragged over to the Works. The nameplates had already been taken off and securely stored. Once having removed all of the fittings, I hid then away, securely locking the doors from prying eyes. The former beauty was then placed over on the back road, out of the way. Hoping

T9	30732	5th February
O2	30224	11th February
O2	30233	19th February
G6	30162	28th February
M7	30038	6th March
N15	30738	13th March
M7	30675	21st March
0395	30568	14th April
0395	30564	26th April
T9	30284	5th May
M7	30022	12th May
H2	32424	26th May
M7	30037	6th June
T9	30285	21st June
H15	30334	13th July
M7	30243	27th September
E1	32113	11th October
T9	30737	18th October

30774, the former 'Sir Gaheris', mantled by snow, in which condition Eric was involved in its dismantling.

against hope, we both waited for the faint chance of an appeal to preserve this once fine locomotive. To put off the inevitable, I would go over to the sheds to see the charge hand fitter, Jimmy Gibson, who would allocate another unfortunate loco for scrapping. Jimmy's was the task of procuring engines from the dump. To him fell the decision as to which loco was next in line to suffer the cutter's torch. I also recorded the numbers of all the locomotives that he dismantled. These were put into three small books, two of which survive to this day. The entries for 1958 are as shown in the table on the previous page.

All the scrapping was on piecework, with a price given for dismantling and cutting a particular class of loco. All that remained for us to do was to come in under the quoted time and we were in profit. As an added bonus, to supplement the basic wage there was regular overtime. At that period the only outside help we received was from the yard gang. These men performed any boiler lifting that was required, using the Royce overhead gantry crane. With the accelerating demise of steam, the early nineteen sixties saw the cutting of locomotives stepped up and a couple of fitters were drafted in to help. Two names I recall from that time were 'Nobby' Clark who was a cutter, and an ex-Ashford man with the nickname of 'Yogi Bear'.

I was still working outside during the 'Big Freeze' of 1963, which lasted nearly three months. During that time the temperature rarely rose above zero. Undeterred, and despite protestations from the management, we continued to work outside. On one occasion our boss called me into the office and forcefully said, "You will have to come in." Too placate him, I proffered a compromise, "O.K. I will come in, when we have got rid of what we've got over here." But then, as

the number of locos diminished, I quietly went over to the running shed to see Jimmy Gibson. Having explained that I did not want to work inside, I requested that a couple more engines should be wheeled over to the scrap yard and out of the sight from the prying eyes of the boss. With great discretion, Jimmy obliged, so I never did have to go into the Works. There was a bonus too, as I never had a cold for the whole of that bitterly winter. I was as fit as a fiddle.

Around this time, the rear of the Works was reorganised for the pending change of work. Instead of constructing and rebuilding steam engines, it would now be maintaining the new diesel locomotives and units in first class mechanical and electrical conditions. Accordingly, numbers one and two bays were refurbished and converted into a dust free environment, for the stripping and rebuilding of the power plants and components.

As part of the general clearing process, an LSW brake body was offered as a replacement for the old mess hut. This we gladly accepted and it was duly brought over to the scrap yard by the breakdown crane. As the old structure was lifted away, two long hidden plates were discovered. The first came from a King Arthur, *Sir Kay*, whilst the second was an Andrew Barclay works plate from the dock loco, *The Master General.* The normal practice when a set of plates had been removed was for them to be taken over to a hut near the Works, where they were restored. For this quarter of a mile trip, a barrow truck was utilised. Once returned to their former glory, the plates went into the stores for safe keeping until disposal.

Returning to the reorganization at the rear of the Works; it had been here that the refurbished steam boilers were tested, but now this same area would be used for

B4, 30093 attended to by the breakdown crane from the nearby running shed. It had become derailed whilst being moved during dismantled. 30093 had been withdrawn in April 1960.

diesel engine testing. For transporting these, a 'King Arthur' tender was stripped and converted to a mobile test plant. Unfortunately every time it was necessary to bring this converted tender round to the back of the Works, it entailed coming through the scrap line, so a lot of reorganizing was required. On one occasion numerous dead locos had to be pulled out, including an H15 and a B4 tank. Both condemned engines had already had their brake rigging torched prior to this move. To begin with all went well as they were unceremoniously dragged out, but when they were pushed back the diminutive tank's rigging fell down and fouled the line, resulting in a derailment. To restore the engine to the track, recourse was made to the breakdown crane which had to come over from the running sheds for the purpose. Eventually, this time consuming exercise came to an end and a purpose built testing plant was constructed.

The scrap lines also played host to a couple of railtours. On one memorable occasion, 'City of Truro' paid a visit to the Works at the head of an Ian Allen special. To return to the shed the engine had to pass over

one of the scrap lines, after which it could gain access to the South Yard and eventually the running shed.

Speaking of nameplates, I recall enquiring at Swindon as to the availability of certain nameplates. My first attempt was to purchase the 'Duke' class plate *Comet*, but to no avail. Next choice was *Ivanhoe*, but again this had already been disposed of as had *County of Hants*. Fortunately, though, one of the plates from *Winchester Castle* was available and I purchased this for the princely sum of fifteen pounds.

At that time I was working in the running sheds and I recall being notified that I had seven days in which the deal on the nameplate was to be closed. Had I failed to find the money it would have been offered to the next person on the list. The plate duty arrived by train, wrapped in hessian, all for a two shillings and sixpence delivery charge. The plate was sold on several years later.

As was the norm, I was working overtime on Saturday morning 18th of May 1963. This was the day that Alan Peglar's newly preserved A3 class Pacific, *Flying Scotsman* was working an enthusiasts' train to

Southampton. I informed the charge hand that I was going over to the running sheds to photograph the train as it passed through, which he readily agreed was O.K.. What I did not know was that the special was running over one hour behind schedule, so I took the opportunity to additionally photograph various other passing trains. These included a passenger working behind Battle of Britain class No 34064 *Fighter Command*, followed by a down empty tanker train to Fawley behind Urie tank No 30517. After this was a local goods working, hauled by an Ivatt 2-6-2 tank, known locally as a 'Teddy Bear'. Such was the variety of motive power and traffic in those far off times. Eventually *'Scotsman* did come through and it was duly photographed, although instead of getting back to the Works before mid day to clock off, it was now 1pm. In those days, the overtime rate was time and a quarter and I booked the requisite extra hours pay. Surprisingly, nobody ever questioned the extra hour. Another rare interloper at that period was A4 Pacific 'Kingfisher' on another special working. This was the only time I witnessed a train departing for Southampton from the south end of Eastleigh up platform.

At the end of a long, hard working day, the most

convenient train home to Winchester was via the DNS. This was also a far more relaxed route than by the Southern main line, especially during the late 1950s. At that time 3440 *City of Truro* was shedded at Didcot, and would invariably be found working the afternoon service home, from Southampton.

Apart from the normal work carried out at Eastleigh on working steam engines, the works also had the task of restoring the last surviving example of William Adams final class of 4-4-0 express passenger engines, No 563, dating from 1893. Built at the then Nine Elms works it was originally withdrawn in 1939, although such were the wartime locomotive shortages that it was put back into traffic. Withdrawn for a second time in 1945, it had been rusting away at Eastleigh until 1948. 1948, though, had been the year of the Waterloo Centenary exhibition and it was decided that No.563 should be restored. A very worthwhile exercise was carried out, including refitting a stove pipe chimney, brass number plates, and returning this fine locomotive to it's former LSWR livery. With the setting up of The Museum of Transport at Clapham, it was fitting that No.563 should be a prime exhibit. For that purpose, the

Eric, on top of the smokebox, with a colleague in the process of dismantling a 'Yankee tank' at the back of the works in May 1962. This was the first of the class to be withdrawn in the same month as cutting took place and was the result of collision damage.

loco entered Eastleigh Works, where it was to be refurbished to exhibition standard.

Mark Abbott, who had been a premium apprentice, was put in charge of the project whilst I was given the task of implementing the mechanical restoration, all of which was performed on overtime. That meant basically that I was the one doing all the dirty work. One evening a group of painters appeared, and duly started working on the wheels. "That dark green is nice, is that the undercoat?" I asked. "Oh no, this is the finish",' said one of the painters. "You have got that wrong, Mate," I retorted, "Well that's what we have got to do," came the reply. What they were doing, of course, was painting the engine 'Goods Green', a 'Holly Green'. I said no more and he carried on with his work. But I did write to John Scholes, then the Curator at Clapham Museum and remarked that the T3 Class was being painted in holly green, which was the LSWR goods colour. Can this be right? I had always been led to believe that the livery for Adams passenger locomotives was 'Pea Green', with black and white lining, as like the fine model on display in the Science Museum. I thought no more about the matter, until one day when I had just returned from lunch and Les Norris came over, with a concerned look on his face. He explained that the foreman, Mr Beesley, wanted a word with me in his office. "What have you been doing?" Mr Beesley asked in a very concerned voice. "I don't know what you are referring to," I replied in a slightly bemused fashion. "Did you write a letter to Mr Scholes?" With that question my eyes lit up and I immediately warmed to the meeting. "Oh, yes, I did. What happened about that?" Mr Beesley did not reply directly, but instead I was told very sternly to go to the main offices, where Mr Stone, who was in charge of the Drawing Office, wished to see me. Mr Stone having recently taken over the drawing office from Mr Mills.

The Drawing Office was outside the main works and consisted of a large brick building fronting the works yard on one side and the main running lines on the other. Once within his office, without so much as a pleasantry being exchanged, Mr Stone exclaimed, "What's this about paint?" I repeated that the engine was being painted in the wrong colour. "How do you know?" asked Mr Stone. Here was my chance for the definitive reply, "Many years ago, in the days of Mr Adams, a model was built by two brothers, which is now on display in the Science Museum. The only thing wrong with it is that the engine was built before the tender. They carry slightly different shades of green." "What colour is it?" asked an extremely vexed Mr Stone. "Pea green", I responded. With that Mr Stone telephoned the paint shop foreman, 'Chippy' Miller. "I have got a man here who says that you are painting an engine the wrong colour!" I could hear the reply for myself, "…Oh Christ, you've got him, have you?" I was trying desperately to suppress a fit of the giggles as I knew full well what was coming next from Mr Stone. "Have you varnished it yet?' "No", replied the paint shop foreman. "If we varnish it, it will make it darker", came the nervous stutter. "We will see about this then" were Mr Stone's final words concerning the colour of No.563 and I left the office hardly able to stop myself from laughing.

Shortly afterwards I was again summonsed by Mr Stone who asked if there were any other things wrong with the restoration in hand. I had a list Mark Abbott had left for me, as Mark had by now moved on to another role. "For a start, they have fitted ordinary BR standard plugs. They are not right, because Adams' plugs had bigger heads on them". Back on the shop floor, the task of restoring the vintage 4-4-0 continued. All of the plugs were removed whilst replicas of the original variety were manufactured in the brass shop. Far from being unhappy about having to make these, the brass shop men were put on overtime to manufacture these special items. In the mean time, the painters completed their repaint, although the final finish, including the intricate lining out, was eventually carried out at Clapham Museum. It had been envisaged that the loco would be towed up to London, but a severe landslide at Winchfield put paid to that plan. The alternative plan saw No 563 towed to Old Town Quay, within Southampton Docks, where it was put onto a Pickfords heavy trailer. Unfortunately the tight curves within the Docks caused substantial damage to the bogie wheel splashers.

A further museum restoration followed the Adams 4-4-0, that of *Boxhill*, a diminutive 'A1' Class 0-6-0 tank engine, constructed by the LBSCR in 1880. Having spent many years as the works shunter at Brighton, it was finally withdrawn in 1946. Fortunately, that same year, it was restored to it's original Stroudley livery and exhibited at the Waterloo Station Centenary celebrations. Before arriving at Eastleigh, *Boxhill* had been stored for many years at a number of locations. At one time it was berthed inside the EMU shed at Farnham, accompanied by No. 563. At Eastleigh Works it was brought into number two bay, which by this time was one of the supposedly, dust free, diesel bays. There are

Opposite page, two more once proud locomotives meet their ends in the scrapyard behind the works at Eastleigh. Above is 30860, once named 'Lord Hawke', built at Eastleigh in April 1929 and withdrawn in August 1962. The photograph was taken by Eric in the following month. Below is 'H16' No 30519, the first of the class to be built, again at Eastleigh, in April 1928. It was withdrawn, along with three other members of the five strong class, in November 1962 and cut up at the back of the works in the same month.

Another once proud steed, redundant and awaiting dismantling. 30937 still retains its smokebox numberplate even though the name 'Epsom' has been removed. This was one of 19 members of the class withdrawn at the stroke of pen in December 1962, thus rendering the type extinct. The photograph was taken in June 1963. 'M7' 30112 alongside had similarly been withdrawn in February 1962. It will be noted that at this time withdrawn engines still displayed evidence of previous cleaning, unlike to all pervading filth that would follow.

photographs extant of this locomotive standing in number two bay awaiting restoration. On the dull paintwork can be seen the name 'Bert Boxhall.' Some wag having noticed the similarity in names. (Bert was the lead fitter in Sid White's gang at that time). When *Boxhill* came to Eastleigh it had accumulated a significant amount of rust and it goes without saying, that the new custodians of the 'dust free' area did not take kindly to my recourse to various grinding tools. A short while later, on a Sunday morning's overtime, I put all of the motion up, although no sooner had I completed this task, than along came another worker who knew better (shades of 563 in reverse!). "All of that has got to come down." "Why?" I enquired. I was then told it had to be painted. Believing I was right, I responded, "You don't paint motion", whereupon I was politely told, "Yes you do, it should be red."

The motion was again removed and the painters went to work on all of the components excepting the connecting rods. The following Sunday was spent repeating that of the previous one and the motion was

hung again. This was the only engine that I ever managed to put the con rods on by myself, so light were the components. As for my colleague, who had spotted the error, the week previously, he was right. I presume that he had seen *Gladstone* and had definitely done his homework. Once all of the work had been completed, *Boxhill* was removed from number two bay and towed over to the coal depot, from where it went off to Clapham by rail.

Away from special work and back to the mundane; the importance of the 'Bosh' was mentioned earlier and with maintenance carried out during the bank holidays. One of theses tasks involved the condenser and was carried out four times a year. This role was always a bone of contention between Les Norris's gang and the millwrights, as the latter men used to complain that their rightful job was being stolen. Another maintenance task concerned the actual boiler. This had the dual role of providing hot water for the Bosh, and also for general washing purposes within the Works. With hard water prevalent in the Eastleigh area, the boiler would have a regular build up of scale. One cold Easter, the cast iron cover was found to have split round the flange. This put the equipment out of action for nearly a fortnight. A brand new component had to be manufactured by the boiler plate fabrication department, following which, the machine shop completed the task. At times such as this, a loco was harnessed as a stationary boiler

On another occasion, this time an August Bank holiday, the gang was again performing their periodic maintenance on the Bosh. At the start of the day, Les Norris told the gang in general conversation how he had just completed building a pond in his garden at home. He then commented, "I want some fish." I replied with the obvious, "Buy them." Les was back, quick as a flash, "Yes, but I've heard that there are some gold fish over in the Carriage Works. I'll tell you what we will do. We will walk over there and have a look later on." In the yard of the Carriage Works was a large water tank, the purpose of which was to provide a reserve supply of water in case of an outbreak of fire in the adjacent timber yard. Consequently later on all of the gang ambled over to the tank and, sure enough, there were numerous huge gold fish, all contentedly swimming round. It was decided to mount a clandestine operation the following day to stock Les's pond.

Consequently, the whole gang finished our allotted task by lunch time, after which it was back over to the water tank. All of that sunny afternoon was fruitlessly spent feeding these huge, spoilt fish. We never did manage to catch one although that was not really surprising. They were fed continuously throughout the week by all of the workers and consequently were not very hungry by the weekend.

'City of Truro' and the journey home via the DNS route have already been mentioned but, after the famous engine was moved away it was the more usual 22xx type that replaced it. Leaving Eastleigh, the first four and a half miles northwards from Eastleigh entailed a steady climb until turning off the main line at Shawford Junction. Usually we had three, sometimes four coaches and on one occasion a 'Pannier Tank' appeared at the head of the train, presumably the booked loco on the down working had failed and the only available engine was commandeered.

Waiting on the platform with me to return home were numerous colleagues who were collectively moaning at the ability of the diminutive tank engine that was to take them home. The day in question was either a Tuesday or a Thursday - boat train days.

Our service was due to depart almost exactly at the time the Waterloo boat train was booked to pass through the station, running on the up main whilst we took the parallel, local line. This invariably resulted in the Western crew racing their illustrious cousin all of the way to the end of the four-track section at Shawford Station.

I stifled the moans from my mates by insisting, "you ain't seen nothing". Sure enough, they went for it, the boat train well on its way, running non-stop through the station whilst the local was still stationary at the platform. Fortunately the road had already been given and as the guard gave the right away, the engine was put into forward gear and the regulator lever opened, the brakes having already been released. Once the tank engine had found it's feet, the driver open it up. The unfortunate fireman must have been working like a slave, as his fire started to go up the chimney whilst the blast from the chimney reverberated in the way that epitomized all Great Western locos. The front of the pannier tank rocked from side to side, as the speed of the thrashed loco steadily increased. Eventually the boat train was caught up and overtaken, much to our delight, although victory would be short lived as we were held by signals at Shawford, the other, far more important working always having priority. Whilst this had been an exemplary run, the 22xx's would invariably put on a good show. It was a mixture of things, competitive spirit and a 'David and Goliath' contest, an outmatched 0-6-0 taking on a 'Lord Nelson' or 'Bulleid Pacific'. In fairness to the Southern, it should be mentioned that these boat trains were never amongst the elite of fast running workings.

By 1964 the works was already in decline, so with the opportunity for redundancy I left the railway in 1964. The choice was simple, leave then whilst there were still jobs available elsewhere, or wait until the rumoured four hundred redundancies occurred, at which time the chances of finding work would almost certainly have been limited. Indeed, the shop stewards were constantly telling the various members of the staff they should try and find a job outside of the railway. Steam was coming to an end, no new locomotives having been constructed at Eastleigh for many years whilst the decision had been taken that no more Bulleid Pacifies were to be rebuilt. More significantly, the influx of dieselisation was in full swing.

Tasker's, the lorry trailer manufacturers, were recruiting fitters at that time. The wages were good, especially when compared to those on the railways, so I applied and was taken on. At first the wages were superb, although unfortunately, after approximately six months the contract for manufacturing trailers for British Road Services came to an end and so did the high wages!

There was only one course left, I applied for the post of a maintenance fitter at Eastleigh Sheds, which fortunately was readily granted. By rights I should not have been working there, because I had what is called on the railway, 'colour defective eyesight'. As a result I was not allowed anywhere out on the track,

All is not quite what it seems. The smokebox number may display 34043, but it is in fact 34055 with a replacement smokebox door, seen in use at Eastleigh as a stationary boiler for repaired safety valves. 34055 had been one of the first three 'Light Pacifics' to be withdrawn in June 1963, the month before the view was taken, the third engine was No 34035. The former 34055 had ceased working due a cracked middle cylinder, which may well account for the missing access plate under the smokebox.

away from the immediate environs of the shed. I was classified as a 'day worker', meaning that Saturday mornings were classed as overtime, which was not the case for the shift workers. I came under the command of Bill Warring, foreman in charge of the fitters.

Despite the fact that steam still had two years left, the run down of Eastleigh Shed was in full swing when I commenced working there in 1965. The depot had been transferred into Nine Elms district on the 30th September 1963. Conditions within were filthy. Squalid would be a better description. Steam depots were never the cleanest of environments to work in, although, at least in Victorian times, they would have been continually swept, ash pits emptied, and the general surroundings kept tidy.

What machinery there was in the shed, was very old. There was a shaper, two lathes and a vertical drill, whilst most of the hand work was performed on aged benches that were well past their days of glory. So primitive were the conditions, that the boiler smiths never had a lobby, Bill Bishop and his chums having recourse to an ancient stove, that was kept continually alight, and

a couple of wooden benches upon which to rest their weary bodies as they ate their food, all in the confines of the filthy, smoky environs of the shed. Fortunately the fitters fared better, as we had the comparative luxury of our own lobby.

Work was restricted to the remaining Bulleid types, Standard classes and the odd visitor. On the Standard's there were drip valves fitted to the vacuum system. The lowest point was where the residue of water in the pipes collected. Here was a simple valve arrangement, which had a rubber ball as it's main element. As soon as a vacuum was created, the ball would rise up and the liquid escape from the system. It was a common chore for the fitters to replace these balls. Once completed, invariably they were not disposed of, as the prime function of these would be to enliven the meal breaks within the lobby. As we all sat around, blissfully eating their food, some comedian could almost be guaranteed to enter the sanctum and cause mayhem. One good heavy throw of the rubber ball, would see it continue to bounce from surface to surface. All the while, the men inside would be cursing as they tried to grab their sandwiches and cups of tea, before they ended on the floor. Better still was when a couple of the lads decided to throw three or four of these missiles in unison!

One Saturday, in early January 1965, we had a batch of LMS locos appear on the shed. These consisted of numerous examples of Stanier 8f 2-8-0's, and one solitary Jubilee 4-6-0. The 8F's were to enter the Works for overhaul, but not so the Jubilee, *Galatea* which still displayed its nameplates. As a precaution against theft, these were removed for safe keeping. Strange as it might seem, the Jubilee had been towed down to Hampshire, with it's rods still on. As the lubrication could have not been working, the speed of travel should not have exceeded twenty five miles per hour although without a shadow of a doubt, the latter speed restriction had not been adhered to. Removing the rods, which was an overtime job, took place one Saturday. I was assisted by my permanent mate, Bill Housego. Jimmy Gibson worked the 45 ton crane. This heavy crane had been transferred to the shed the previous year, having replaced DS35. Various improvements over it's predecessor included the automatically applied jib brake and a higher boiler pressure of 120 lbs. 'Galatea' was wheeled onto number three road so that the pit could be utilised. The middle rods were disconnected and dropped onto the base of the pit. This was followed by a great deal of physical effort, dragging them out from under the front buffer beam. Then the crane lifted these and the outside rods into the tender. Within a short period of time, *Galatea* was dragged off, unceremoniously, to Barry scrapyard. Fortunately it was to survive the cutter's torch and find it's way into preservation.

Readers will recall my comment over the Bulleid 'Pacific' type. Now I was in a position to confirm that first impression, not always in the politest terms. They were supposed to have a wealth of labour saving features, which would mean a ready welcome from the running department, but something went wrong somewhere. When working on the unrebuilt type, the oil bath was the most disliked part as far as most fitting staff were concerned. This was especially so when we had to actually go inside the thing. Firstly, the large and very awkward sump casing had to be removed. This bulky component was secured by fifty plus studded bolts. Between the two surfaces was a very large gasket, all of which was located above the centre axle. But before removal the bath had to be drained of it's forty gallons of oil. Not that this task would stop us becoming totally plastered within a very short space of time. Consider also all of the internal components, including the chain, which would still be dripping oil for days to come!

We had to get up inside that lot, including the three row crank, all constantly dripping oil. Then somehow we had to work inside. Access to the middle piston was like a submariner trying to get a jammed torpedo out of a tube. Despite the apparent external bulk of the engines, inside the oil bath the width was less than a man's shoulders, which resulted in him becoming soaked through with this dirty, smelly and very sticky substance.

As a comparison take a much older design, the Brighton I1 4-4-2T. Here the gap between the frames was 4ft. 1 in. On a Bulleid in was 3ft. 6in. In his infinite wisdom, Mr Bulleid had decided to place the axle boxes in the middle of the frames - which is sound in theory. Unfortunately very real problems arose in practice. With so much muck around the working area, the oil bath, it was very difficult to get into the confined space to remove one.

Then we had another little job. Running along the inside of the air smooth casing was a bank of copper pipes. This comprise approximately ten in total and all came from the lubricator. In time the metal became hard and split and it would be necessary to replace one. If these were nice and clean there would have been no problem, but inside the casing they were smothered in muck thrown up from the track. Some poor unfortunate would have to climb onto the front of the loco and pump away at the lubricators. In theory this should have revealed the offending split, but it was not always so obvious due to the liberal coating of oil and grime. We could spend ages mucking about in all that mess before finally tracing the split.

Another common problem was with the clacks, again on the inside of the casing and situated at the top of the loco. Access was gained via a removable panel, behind which and all around the working area, was a mass of fibreglass lagging. Due to the heat within the area, after a time this lagging would break up. In doing so, it made the task of working there very dusty and dirty. To make matters worse, all the work on these components had to be performed whilst standing on a ladder. As well as being awkward, it was also very tiring on the legs.

Then there was the positioning of the lubricators at the front and below the smokebox. This was always going to be a trap for ashes and dirt. Inside the smokebox and at the bottom were the removable plates that gave access to the front of the inside cylinder. Once removed, many hours of work followed, all carried out by leaning down through this orifice!

The Ql's, Bulleid's wartime 0-6-0 class, were just as bad. Again we had to work off a ladder as there was no running plate. An added problem was the fact that there was nothing to hang on to. These locos had a top feed, so once again any attention required the use of a ladder. Other examples of top feed locomotives were the 'Black Fives' and the very similar 'Standard' classes, although on these the feet were placed on the handrail with his knees firmly pressed onto the boiler side. In this manner we could lean over to the fitting.

Bulleid Pacifies had an automatic blow down. When performing boiler inspections this component had to be removed. The theory was that a colleague could then shine a light through the vacated space to check the inside condition of the firebox plates. Unfortunately and despite all of the trouble involved, very little could be seen within. Basically it was a great deal of hard work for very little return, as the blow down device was a very heavy component. As well as the excessive weight, another dislike was the copper convex ring that was fitted behind the valve. Horrible things! I say that with feeling, as after one particular occasion performing this task I was off sick for three weeks with a bad back.

On another occasion I was repeating this process on West Country class No 34008 'Padstow'. Having refitted the device, I then refilled the boiler to it's very limit. Although not my job to do so, I wanted to check that all of the joints were thoroughly tight. As far as I was concerned, everything was now as it should be as nothing appeared to be leaking. The following morning, Jim Gibson, the chargehand fitter, informed me that I was wanted in the foreman's office, right away. "Oh yeah, what's up then?", I asked. Jim replied that he did not know, so over to the offices I sauntered, feeling very bemused to say the least. The offices were situated within a very substantial brick building, on top of which was the shed's vast water tank. Through the main doorway and up the first flight of stairs I went, all the while trying to think of anything that might have gone amiss, but absolutely nothing came readily to mind.

As soon as I had entered the Foreman's office, and without so much as a good morning exchanged, Mr. Hayle angrily tore into me. "Are you the fitter that was working on '34' yesterday?" "Yes", came my very short, but guarded response. "What kind of a fitter are you?" Still totally puzzled at what was wrong, I replied, "What's the matter. What's the problem?" "They had to cancel a train yesterday because 'Padstow' failed". Still only just a little bit the wiser, I asked the obvious question. "Why?" "Because they said the blow down valve had leaked!" Retaliating now and knowing full well that all my work the previous day had been fully double checked by myself, I angrily retaliated. "I know nothing about that. When I filled the b....r up with water it was alright. I can't fill it up and light the thing, so I don't know. I can't do more than that!" I must have made my point clearly, as Mr. Hayles then softened his tone and dismissively replied, "Alright then" and so brought the meeting to a close.

All this time I was also suffering a severe distraction, as besides looking the boss straight in the eye, I was also looking at a fine, large photograph that adorned the wall behind the desk. This was of 'Schools' class 4-4-0 No.900 Eton, in Works grey! It was just a case of getting my priorities right!

Mr Hayle was on the verge of retirement at this time, finally vacating his office in November 1966. The new incumbent was Mr Dale, who came from Salisbury shed. Unfortunately for him, steam was in it's final death throws, so he was unable to make any personal impression on how he would have liked the place to be run. A change at the top there may have been, but one piece of continuity still existed, Cyril Stephens still retained his position as the assistant shed master.

One other piece of continuity was also guaranteed, as far us unfortunate fitters were concerned, namely the joys of working on the despised unrebuilt Pacifies. 34064 *Fighter Command* was one of these. As late as 1962 this loco had been fitted with a narrow chimney, that was so characteristic of the Giesel Oblong ejector experiment. In total there were seven nozzles, plus blower jets between, all of which blew the exhaust up through the chimney in a narrow line. Although a relative success, a scheme to fit twenty more such locos was not instigated.

This particular loco chimney was cast iron, the base of which had a large flange, which had broken away. Before the problem could be rectified, the heavy chimney would have to be lifted from the smokebox. Unknown to me was the fact that the shed's roof struts were of different sizes. The loco was placed under one such fitting, a block and tackle swung over, the chimney successfully extricated. No sooner had the task been accomplished then along came Jimmy Gibson, who promptly explained that I could have pulled the roof down as we had not used a load bearing truss.

A final example of working on an unrebuilt example typifies all that was wrong with these engines. On this occasion it had been reported that the steam reverser was playing up. Old Bert Warring said to me, "…That will take about a day and a half." I got underneath and undid the plate at the back. Inside was not oil but water. I managed to remove the pin for the buckle that linked the component to the valve gear, after which Bert explained to me that there was an eye bolt somewhere there. This appeared completely out of sight. "By sticking a stop through there you should be able to get the steam reverser down," was his next piece of advice. For all of my efforts, I could not locate the eye bolt. There was just not one there. There was no alternative, so up inside I had to squeeze my torso between the boiler and the casing. By that time I was smothered in muck that had been thrown up there from the wheels and the brakes. In the end it took four days to get that reverser out. Everything was rusted solid, where large coatings of water, oil, and muck had condensed and emulsified. For all of my troubles, despite also the effort I had put in, Bert moaned like hell at the time that I had taken on this evil chore.

There were constant rumours about the impending closure of Eastleigh shed. As staff departed for better paid jobs, they were never replaced and the inevitable cycle of decline escalated. Steam locomotives were being withdrawn at that time, often because of quite minor and easily repaired problems.

On one particular occasion I was performing the role of the examination fitter whilst working a twelve hour shift. A message was relayed to me that 'Merchant Navy' class No.35005 *Canadian Pacific* had a suspected moving tyre on one of it's driving wheels. To prove the point, prior to running off of Nine Elms depot, the offending wheel had a vertical line chalked onto the tyre. When it came onto Eastleigh shed, I had to inspect the wheel. Sure enough the single line was now composed of two shorter ones, proving that there was indeed movement. Accordingly the loco was withdrawn from traffic. The one and only time I had the distinction of taking a loco permanently out of service.

The pending closure of the shed was all too clear at that time. I first tried to get a transfer onto the new form of traction, but to no avail. The reason given my colour defective eyesight. With different coloured piping and cable runs on the new diesels, it was assumed I would be unable to perform the new tasks. Escape came via a job at the nearby Ford's factory, as I did not want to wait until the final demise. Ironically my colour deficiency was not unique, as it was found out at the eleventh hour that a considerable number of the breakdown gang had had the same problem for many years!

19th May 1967 was a black day as far as the shed's mechanical staff were concerned, for on that memorable day, all those remaining were given six weeks notice of redundancy. Come the fateful day, which occurred on the 9th of July, the final fires were dropped and steam was no more.

Perhaps my final comment would be as follows. If I should ever come into a large sum of money, I will buy an unrebuilt Bulleid pacific. Once fully restored I will then take great delight in cutting it into very small and useless pieces, which I will give to any poor soul that professes to like these infernal machines!

45699 'Galatea' alongside what was by this time a very decrepit coaling stage at Eastleigh, January 1965. This was the engine referred to, which arrived at the shed 'dead', but complete with rods and nameplate intact. Withdrawn from Shrewsbury it was moved from Eastleigh to Barry, ostensibly for scrap, but was subsequently rescued for preservation.

All photographs Eric Best collection

Following on from Graham Hatton's piece on Weedkilling Trains (pages 77-79 'SW' Issue 2) and the Relaying at Waterloo feature from the same issue, Alan Blackburn has provided a further instalment of fascinating notes:

"No mention of the Southern's Weed Killing trains would be complete without mention of the Civil Engineer's Weed Killing Train Inspector, Charles Richards. One remembers Charlie as a quiet neat little man who rarely came into the office. He had two or three claims to fame, he was the first and last Weed Killing Train Inspector, having had charge of the first of these trains back in 1931, the second formed in 1936 and the last featured in my old colleague Graham's article in 1949. He continued with this train until sometime in the late 1960's, when he retired and the work was handed over to Messrs Chipman to be carried out by contract. I remember that for a year or two a portion of Charlie's train was retained to do the Hastings line, as the Chipman's train was out of gauge for this route, a problem that was solved when some of the tunnels were re-built. One of Charlie's other claims to fame was that he was almost certainly the only man who had traveled over every mainland Southern Railway running line, every actual line, that is, not just the routes, with the exception of the Lynton & Barnstable. (The Island, they had their own train and looked after their own affairs.) It followed that Charlie's knowledge of the railway was truly unique. He not only had charge of the train when it was in use, but he was also responsible for the maintenance of the trains pumping and spraying equipment, which was accommodated in the end "U" van. The second van in the train was his living vehicle which he used, not only when the train was out spraying but frequently when it was berthed. It's original home was in Blackheath sidings but latterly it went to Horsham.

"In the photo taken on the Isle of Grain incidentally, one can just see Charlie looking out of the offside window and controlling the Cess sprays which could be swung in or out as required. In the centre window can be seen the Guard, who was in communication with the Driver by means of a simple electric bell circuit. Looking out of the nearside window and controlling the Cess sprays on that side would be the local Permanent Way Inspectors representative or possibly an assistant, although by the time I knew Charlie he did not have one.

"Graham rightly mentions the complexities of the Special Traffic arrangements needed each year and it was said by those concerned that they were by far the most difficult job in the office. Many of those were railway enthusiasts and they got their reward by being taken out for a day on the train, invariably on one of those days when it penetrated some branch line, long closed to passenger traffic. In later years I was responsible for the weed killing trains activities and, strangely enough, I too found it convenient to travel on these branch line days. One day, I remember, we were headed off down the Fawley branch when some chap in a field exposed himself to us. He had not, however, counted on the reach of the manually operated bank-side spray and got one hell of a shock!

"One last recollection of later years was a prohibition of locomotives from working over the South London Line. That did not stop us running the weed killing train over these lines though, we had it hauled by two of the CME's Snow and Ice units, whilst the engine ran through from London Bridge to Victoria via another route. I felt sure someone would take a photo of these events but I never saw one published.

"Turning again to Graham's article on the Waterloo relaying, the first two photos show the Mitcham Fitting Up Ground (Mitcham FUG). In the early 1960's this work and the men associated with it were transferred to Woking where, of course, they were still known as the Mitcham Gang. Things did not always go according to plan and I remember asking Tom Thomas, who was their Inspector in charge, what his most difficult situation had been. He told me how, one early morning up at Waterloo, he had knocked the gang off for tea whilst, as was his habit, he had a quiet look round to see that all was well. Imagine his shock then when he looked up from some detail to see the lead heading towards the platform ramp instead of some feet to one side of it. Having put aside his first thought, to get someone senior out of bed, he realised the only person who could get the job finished on time was him! Tom had built a lot of S&C in his time and he knew his geometry. Luckily the job was a Bullhead one and he realised that if he crowed the "fronts", that is the portion of switch between the first set of fishplates and the switch tips, he could get things back to more or less to where they should be. He did this and that was an end to the matter, until the first Class 50 arrived at Waterloo one morning, a good many years later and promptly became derailed as it was about to enter the platform.

"Senior people were not happy and yours truly was dispatched to Waterloo to see what had happened. It was not that the Chief did not trust the Division to tell him in their own good time, but rather that he had to explain the event to the General Manager within an hour or so. Well, to cut a long and not uninteresting story short and despite the fact that literally tens of thousands of train movements had traversed Tom's handy-work successfully, including of course the largest of steam locomotives, the fact was that a class 50 derailment could not we put down to bogie rotational stiffness. We immediately put a ban on the Class 50's from using the same route and the point was proved for us the next day when the new restriction was overlooked and we had a second 50 on the dirt in exactly the same spot!

John Morgan in charge of the Switch and Crossing design, was determined to get to the bottom of what had happened and referring back to the original site notebooks and their calculations, which were always kept, he found that the survey had been started by one person and for some reason finished by another. Unfortunately one had used the corner of a certain relay case as a datum whilst his successor had used another close by. There was nothing wrong with the drawing and the layout which resulted, except, as Tom found out the hard way, it would not fit the site. You can just see an earlier version of the points in question to the left of locomotive 34011 on page 49." (Southern Way No 2.)

Above - Weed killing on the Isle of Grain, 7th April 1949, referred to in the accompanying text. The locomotive is No 33039.

Above - A view we did not use in Issue 2 purely because of space. Clearly South Eastern (ish) but any clues about the location would be welcome. (I can see the subject of weed killing continuing to grow……..!)

Permanent Way Notes by Graham Hatton

Third Rail Items on the Southern

This is the first of a short series on items associated with the conductor rail. The Southern was not unique in using a third 'live' rail for propulsion of trains, but it soon became the largest user on British Railways. In other parts of the country such as Newcastle, Liverpool and the Watford DC (Direct Current) system, the components, rails and power supply system developed along similar lines, but there were differences of detail. Some trains for the Watford system were even built by the Southern. London Transport and its predecessors developed a similar propulsion system to suit their needs, but they opted for a fourth rail system, the negative return to the sub-station being via the centre conductor rail and not the running rails.

The Southern had inherited two different electrification systems from its absorbed companies. The LBSCR tried overhead lines at 6,600v AC (Alternating Current) in 1909, to stem losses from the travelling public, to alternative transport, such as trams in the suburban areas, started to take real effect. The LSWR authorised third rail electrification, at 600v DC, for similar reasons in 1913. At the grouping they had 24.5 and 57 route miles electrified respectively, whilst the LSWR also had the isolated 1.5 miles of the Waterloo and City railway. Electrification was able to provide trains which could accelerate quicker compared with previous steam hauled services.

Early on in its existence, the new Southern Railway Company decided to electrify parts of the Eastern section on the DC system and although the AC system had reached Sutton and Coulsdon North on the Central Section, standardisation was the order of the day. DC was then set as the selected policy in 1926 for all running lines.

Expansion was rapid under the dynamic leadership of Sir Herbert Walker. Thus by 1929 there were 277 route miles, equivalent to about 17% of the system where passenger services were worked by electric units. Concurrent with this was the abolition of the former LBSCR overhead although it is still possible to see the ends of some of the cut back supports for the AC system in Clapham Cutting high up on the walls.

This article is only a brief look at the system, starting with the conductor rail and its supports. These were, and still are, a Permanent Way function. Within each P.Way section there would be specialist staff to undertake tasks associated with the conductor rails' installation and connections. Further specialists then carried out cabling and work to connect them and the negative return to the point of power supply in the sub-station.

1

THIRD RAIL ITEMS ON THE SOUTHERN

Photo 2 - This shows a close-up of an anchor pot. These tended to be more sturdily constructed and were often made of glass. The rail clamps are fitted to the rail either side of the pot after installation. They are clipped around the rail foot and fastened with that beloved tool of the P.Way, a big hammer! Without the anchor pots, expansion and the continuous movement of shoes on the rail would in time move the rail along. The anchors were carefully specified and fitted at the middle of the rail length. Fitting too many anchors on rails where excessive movement occurred, particularly on sharp curves, could actually tip the con rail outwards from the pot in hot weather, with the risk of a shoe getting inside the con rail, with further disastrous effect!

Photo 1 - The third rail is energised at between 600 & 750v DC and is a 'non earthed' system relying on a good return path for the current from the trains via the running rails. Good bonding of components is therefore most essential. We will look more carefully at bonding, switches and joining rails in a future article. The third rail is maintained on ceramic insulators or pots 3" above the running rail, the centre of the con rail is 16" to one side of the running rail edge. Pots varied, with four main sizes classified A-D, of which D was a flat one for ramp ends. This allows for the variation in rail height between BH & FB rail and their fastenings, also the difference in con rail size. Originally 100lb / yard rail was used then 106lb and more recently 150lb. Until recently con rail was of iron and so much softer than conventional steel running rails. This was preferred for electrical reasons, lower resistance, but required careful handling by the P.Way! The pot sits on a wooden packing and is fastened by cleats around its base. The rail height is fine tuned by top packing and carefully maintained for lateral positioning as the lightly pressing train collection shoe has no guidance other than being positioned to follow the rail. As the conductor rail is free to expand on the pots as ambient temperatures rise, to avoid excessive movement at its ends its maximum length is limited to about 900ft. At the ends ramps allow the shoe to fall from and rise onto the rail. Typically ramps lengths of 10ft allow this, the vehicle shoe being limited to a drop of just one inch, so that it is able to pass over running rails without arcing. Shorter ramps are used at low speed. In the picture the rear track has the typical, standard ramp. The nearer ramp was experimental at this stage. It allowed the use of standard pots, but also kept the rail up out of standing water that may have pooled on the track in poor weather. For that reason these ramps are known as flood ramps. These ramps are common now, but the picture was taken years ago! Note also the experimental bonding between the con rail ends, as an alternative to the more normal cable bonding around the gap.

THIRD RAIL ITEMS ON THE SOUTHERN

Photo 3.- Borough Market Junction, in 1954. The complexity of the conductor rail is more obvious. On one train, collector shoes are all connected together within a train set, which helps smooth current collection and avoid snatches. Trains can pass over small gaps by momentum, but slow moving trains can become 'gapped', that is to say sat in an area without con rail. Switch and crossing areas have to be carefully designed, as extra gaps are required and rail changes sides, but trains must have a reasonable, and hopefully continuous, power supply. Each gap has a ramp end to the con rail. Where shoes leave or join the side of a rail on a diverging route, a side ramp must be supplied to allow the shoe to rise onto or fall from the main rail. This also includes non electrified track where electric stock might be hauled from, such as sidings.

Short rails, normally referred to as floaters, are provided to try to fill in long gaps in the normal conductor rail, such as at crossover positions. The designer also needs to avoid shoes on adjacent rails coming close to, or touching rail on adjacent lines and thus 'bridging' across between neighbouring track feeds. A track feed to the conductor rail, usually feeds one line on one route. When it is needed to isolate specific lines for engineering reasons, 'bridging' by a train between the live and isolated rails could be very serious for anyone working on the isolated rails. The designer of the layout will reduce the risk of this, but in complex layouts, during times of isolation, any risk has to be considered and further hook switches (localised switches, to be covered later) need to be opened.

In the photo it can be seen that as far as possible the conductor rail is gapped when near point motors, and where rods pass underneath it. It may also need gapping at some metal underbridges, typically subways, and, of course public crossings. Dealing with the three tracks in the foreground, the middle track shows the motor on the left with its associated rods to the point. The con rail has been located on the right. The left hand track shows the conductor rail passing adjacent to the switch on the non motor side. It has a side ramp fitted. The ramp is like a piece of angle section bolted to the main rail and carries the shoe to the point where switch and stock rail running edges are about 8 inches apart before dropping it on a very short ramp. Side ramps were extensively used by the Southern, but the short ramps are undesirable and wear very quickly, so their use is decreasingly popular.

In the middle switch, the con rail on the right hand turnout route resumes at the 8" position, where the paths of shoes on passing trains are deemed to be sufficiently far apart to avoid touching an adjacent rail which is not applicable to the route the train is taking. The rails stop short of the diamond crossing from the left turnout and the middle one, to avoid the bridging issue referred to above. Some third rail areas other than the Southern, for example the L&Y, tried dropping the conductor rail adjacent to a switch to avoid side ramps, the shoe momentarily losing contact with the continuous rail.

Note the wood trunking, specially made to hold the power cables and protect them. Cables in the foreground have made good use of the trough decking of the underbridge (leading to Tower Bridge). The track is on wheel timbers here, longitudinal baulk timbers spanning between and fixed to the steel deck troughs. The cables also run under the motors. All had to be carefully thought out at the design and installation stage.

Borough Market Signal Box is on the right and the actual Market is in the vee of the junction. Waterloo East and Charing Cross are on the left, Cannon Street on the right, with London Bridge Station immediately behind the photographer. This is probably the busiest piece of track on the Southern, particularly the two tracks leading away to the right. Today it is still referred to as 'The Critical' and it certainly is!

Photo 4 - On the SW mainline again, this shows the unusual use of side ramps on each side of a turnout, probably to avoid gapping or excessive arcing issues. Normally con rail on both sides was avoided, but occasionally it had to be considered. Note here, however, the metal point rodding had to pass under the live con rail! This was sufficiently clear in its normal position, but avoided where possible to avoid 'dragging debris', on a shoe, livening things up!

The picture also shows the overlap of con rail, those on the second fast line from the left being unusually long, while the overlap on the third track is more normal. Minimum overlaps between ramp tops were specified in standards, as were many measurements.

Photo 5. - Very occasionally, and particularly in sidings, con rail even extended through foot crossings, though never through public crossings! Staff were expected to understand the implications and lift their feet! Guard boarding would be provided in stations where shunting occurred, in and around pointwork which required it and normally at ramp ends approaching most crossings. It was mostly double sided of 7" x 1.5" treated boarding, 'feathered' at the top edge. It was held away from the actual con rail by brackets and cleats screwed to the sleepers, and fixing screws on the boarding outside! Painting of rail and board ends white varied from area to area but was common in stations so as to highlight the dangers to staff, particularly of live con rail ends or, in this case, to remind staff to tread with care.

We regret that pure pressure of space has meant the Letters page has had to be omitted from this Issue. We do, though, sincerely thank all who have contacted us with comments and additional information both with reference to Issue 3 and to earlier editions.

Space has similarly precluded the inclusion this time of Terry Cole's Rolling Stock feature, but it will re-appear again in No 5.

Alan Blackburn, see pages 90 and 91, has kindly responded to our earlier plea for information on the various carriage sheds that existed, both for electric and loco hauled stock. However, we could still do with more. Can you help please?

Another 'Terrier' to be restored at Eastleigh in the time of Eric Best, see page 82, was the former LBSCR No 54 'Waddon'. Originally built in February 1876, it was transferred to the duplicate list as No 654 in January 1900 and sold to the neighbouring SECR in September 1904 for £670. Under its new owners it became their No 751 retaining this number upon its return to Southern Railway stock in 1923. (according to Bradley, this was the last steamable locomotive to retain SECR grey). After work at Folkestone Quay and as shed pilot at Battersea, it was then placed in store before being used to supply steam for the pulverised coal experiments at Eastbourne until 1932. Next came a period of use as the Lancing Works Shunter, numbered 680S, and in which role it continued at work until June 1962. This was now the end of its operational life as it was taken to Eastleigh and slowly restored as a static exhibit for the Canadian Historic Association. It was shipped from London Docks in August 1963. The illustration depicts the engine in its cosmetically restored state outside the front of Eastleigh Works.

This and the colour illustrations that follow were kindly given to us by Mike Radford. Their origin is uncertain, but some, possibly all, may originate from the former ADC collection.

Opposite upper - 'W' class tank, 31922, clearly displaying a 71A (Eastleigh) shed-plate, yet with the view possibly taken at Feltham. This was one of five members of the class transferred to the Hampshire shed as replacements for the 'H16' type and used on Fawley oil trains, until displaced by diesel traction in November 1962. On paper, at least, the engine survived until August 1963, although it is not certain if it was one of the remaining members of the class that ended their days banking trains between the Western and Southern lines at Exeter.

Opposite lower - 'M7' 30035, for many years a Plymouth based engine, but transferred to Eastleigh in 1960, seen here at what most certainly is Feltham, the predominance of 'Q1's has to be the confirmation.

Above - At an unknown location on the Southern Eastern, (someone will tell us where - *please!*), 30915 'Brighton' heads what may be an Eastbourne special. The coaching stock would appear to increase in status behind the tender, Maunsell, BR Mk 1 and Pullman, whilst the fireman has clearly started firing, by arrangement perhaps?

Issue No 5 of *THE SOUTHERN WAY* (ISBN 978-1-906419-10-3) will be available in January 2009.

Amongst the articles scheduled for inclusion are 'Sam Fay and the LSWR', 'Basingstoke Part 2', and of course 'Permanent Way Notes'.

To receive your copy the moment it is released, order in advance from your usual supplier, or direct from the publisher:

Kevin Robertson (Noodle Books) PO Box 279, Corhampton, SOUTHAMPTON, SO32 3ZX

Tel / Fax 01489 877880

www.kevinrobertsonbooks.co.uk

A clean example of a former SECR 'D1' 4-4-0, possibly at its home depot of Gillingham. This member of the class was overhauled at Ashford between 1958 and 1960, which no doubt contributed to it being retained on the Eastern section after the general demise of steam in 1959 Accordingly, No 31487 along with five others were transferred to Tonbridge for work on Brighton, Eastbourne and Oxted services. This lasted until June 1960, after which it moved to Bricklayers Arms. The engine was finally withdrawn in February 1961.

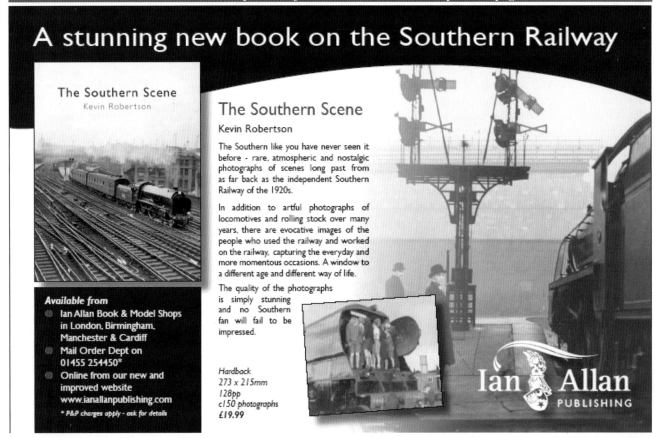